THINNER
IN AN INSTANT
COOKBOOK

THINNER
IN AN INSTANT
COOKBOOK

GREAT-TASTING DINNERS WITH 350 CALORIES OR FEWER—
FROM THE INSTANT POT® OR OTHER ELECTRIC PRESSURE COOKER

Nancy S. Hughes

HARVARD
COMMON
PRESS

Brimming with creative inspiration, how-to projects, and useful information to enrich your everyday life, Quarto Knows is a favorite destination for those pursuing their interests and passions. Visit our site and dig deeper with our books into your area of interest: Quarto Creates, Quarto Cooks, Quarto Homes, Quarto Lives, Quarto Drives, Quarto Explores, Quarto Gifts, or Quarto Kids.

Inspiring | Educating | Creating | Entertaining

First Published in 2019 by The Harvard Common Press, an imprint of The Quarto Group, 100 Cummings Center, Suite 265-D, Beverly, MA 01915, USA.
T (978) 282-9590 F (978) 283-2742 QuartoKnows.com

The Harvard Common Press titles are also available at discount for retail, wholesale, promotional, and bulk purchase. For details, contact the Special Sales Manager by email at specialsales@quarto.com or by mail at The Quarto Group, Attn: Special Sales Manager,100 Cummings Center, Suite 265-D, Beverly, MA 01915, USA.

23 22 21 20 19   1 2 3 4 5

ISBN: 978-1-55832-950-8

Digital edition published in 2019

Library of Congress Cataloging-in-Publication Data available

Design: Rita Sowins / Sowins Design
Photography: Kristin Teig

Printed in China

The information in this book is for educational purposes only. It is not intended to replace the advice of a physician or medical practitioner. Please see your health-care provider before beginning any new health program.

FSC
www.fsc.org

MIX
Paper from responsible sources
FSC® C008047

DEDICATION

To "the Greg." My husband, my best friend . . .
my favorite person ever!

You would walk in the door after your own
"pressured" day to pressure cookers in the sink,
pressure cookers cooking away—everywhere you
look, every surface is covered—and you just roll
up your sleeves and chip in for hours . . . whew.

Thanks for being there . . . always . . . always

CONTENTS

INTRODUCTION

Not one, **not one**, of the healthy pressure cooker recipes in this book is more than 350 calories per serving! Think about it. That means you are able to keep your calories in check without having to constantly tally up! If you want *dinner in an instant* (which is what the Instant Pot and other electric pressure cookers make possible) and wouldn't mind also being *thinner in an instant* (which 350-calorie dishes can help you achieve), you have come to the right place.

The recipes in this cookbook range from a low of 120 calories per serving to 350 calories per serving. Now, that's not just for a small serving of lean meat or a bowl of veggies . . . that's meat and potatoes, one-dish meals, meatless entrées, desserts . . . etc. Get the idea? They never exceed 350 calories . . . *period*!

Calories, if you don't really pay attention, can escalate—and escalate *fast*—before you even realize what's happening. But who likes being told they can't have something they want, like something substantial and filling—and tasty—for dinner? I certainly don't.

So I figure out ways to have it, and have it "within the boundaries." That's *my* job . . . to deliver great tasting recipes within "calorie" boundaries, ones that are fast, high in flavor, easy, and, by the way, economical!

ARE ELECTRIC PRESSURE COOKERS REALLY THAT GREAT?

Electric pressure cookers can keep you from using the excuse "But everything's frozen" or "I'm out of time" to cook at home. Those excuses will pack in the calories when you call for delivery or go through a drive-thru. Learn to rely on your pressure cooker instead. For example, you can . . .

- Start a recipe using frozen vegetables
- Thaw *and* cook frozen ground beef and turkey in a matter of minutes
- Cook solid-as-a-rock frozen boneless skinless chicken breasts in minutes that are t-e-n-d-e-r and juicy without any stringy, chewy, tough results—seriously
- Cook a dish that normally takes hours in a hot oven, or on a back burner that has to be monitored, in a fraction of the time
- Cook dried beans without soaking and serve them in about 35 minutes . . . from dried to table
- Make quick "pressure cooker" croutons and hardboiled eggs to include in a fresh green salad for a meatless entrée (with the promise of easy-peel, zip-off egg shells)
- "Bake" potatoes that actually have the same flavor as those baked in an oven for more than an hour in a fraction of the time

Those are just a few examples to show that electric pressure cookers really are that great!

TYPES OF RECIPES IN THIS BOOK

The varied recipes here include some protein/vegetable combinations, some protein with pasta or rice, while others can be served over veggie spirals, sautéed veggies, or riced veggies as a base, as well as soups, stews, and desserts. No matter what you choose, though, the calories will not exceed that 350-calorie cap!

There's a wide range of recipe types—from Mexican, Italian, and Asian to Middle Eastern, Southern, and all-American—that includes traditional beef stew and the popular ancient grain bowls!

The recipes in this book are designed to serve four. I felt there was a definite need to go that direction with so many smaller households just starting out or downsizing a bit. I found that the majority of electric pressure cooker cookbooks on the market include recipes designed to serve more. There *are* some recipes in this book that serve more than four, but only those that can freeze successfully so you can have them for another meal down the road . . . and they are tagged to let you know that.

SIMPLE INGREDIENTS, SHORT DIRECTIONS

The electric pressure cooker is designed to make cooking fast and more convenient, and to help retain the nutritional benefits of your food, which is all great. But I went a step further and did not include long ingredient lists or complicated, laborious directions to help keep it simple.

The ingredients in these recipes are all mainstream and easily available. There are no special trips to special stores for anything . . . at all!

I've written the directions in a way that will make cooking with an Instant Pot or other electric pressure cooker less intimidating. I was overwhelmed at first (probably like most of you), so I promised myself I would keep that in mind when writing the directions—keeping the recipes simple to follow and even simpler to prep!

Since I don't know what type of electric pressure cooker you own, I've created healthy, low-calorie recipes to work in any standard electric pressure cooker. So whether you have the basic model or the "latest and greatest," you can make these recipes with successful, delicious, and healthy results!

I'm not taking you into every button on the pressure cooker, because each brand is a little different. But they all have a Manual button and a Sauté/Browning button of one sort or another. Since I want to keep things s-i-m-p-l-e, that's *all* I'm using throughout this book for your cooking functions . . . the Manual button and the Sauté/Browning button *only* (and the Cancel button to switch between the two cooking modes).

I'm keeping this simple for you, so you'll be able to make these recipes again and again; after all, isn't that what it's all about? I always say, "if a recipe is difficult or time consuming, you'll make it once in a while (*maybe*), *but* if it's easy and fast, you'll make it . . . and *want* to make it . . . again and again . . . and *that* is what helps you *enjoy* staying on a healthy track!

TIPS, TRICKS, AND HACKS FOR HEALTHY AND LOW-CALORIE PRESSURE COOKING

This chapter provides helpful "Did you know?" bullet points on shopping, ways to add "free" flavor, when to add that free flavor, and how to pack more nutrients into your dishes. It also includes pointers on which kind of small and inexpensive—but *important*—kitchen items will be very useful in making pressure cooking work for you!

EXTRA (VERY MINIMAL) EQUIPMENT NEEDED

- Trivet (generally comes with your pressure cooker)
- Collapsible steamer basket
- 4 (6-oz, or 170 g) custard cups . . . for desserts
- 8-inch (20 cm) nonstick springform pan . . . for desserts
- Food scale . . . for accurate weights of ingredients
- Ruler . . . for measuring ½-inch, ¾-inch, and 1-inch (1, 2, and 2.5 cm) cubes
- Aluminum foil . . . for slings
- 1-quart (946 ml) resealable plastic bags . . . for degreasing
- Paper towels . . . for skinning chicken legs and thighs

POINTERS FOR FAST AND HEALTHY COOKING

- When purchasing bell peppers for stuffing, choose the wider, fatter variety rather than the narrower ones. They're easier to fill and keep their balance better while cooking.
- Watching your carb intake? Pick up a package or two of frozen riced veggies or spiralized veggies . . . or thinly slice low-carb veggies, such as zucchini, yellow squash, or snow peas, and cook a couple of minutes in the microwave to use as a base instead of rice, pasta, or potatoes.

- If you plan to use a large amount of fresh garlic in about a 2-week period, you might want to buy peeled fresh garlic cloves sold in plastic containers in the produce section.
- When shopping for fresh ginger, there is no need to buy a large amount if only a small amount is needed . . . just break off what you need. The general rule is a 1-inch (2.5 cm) piece of fresh ginger yields about 1 teaspoon of grated ginger.
- When buying chuck roast, always buy more than needed for the recipe. Even with lean cuts, there's still a bit of fat to discard.
- To get more bread "surface" when making a sandwich using Italian or French bread, hollow out the center. Halve the bread lengthwise; remove the center portion of the bread, leaving a ½-inch (1 cm) border. You can then fill it with tons of veggies and a bit of lean meat or cheese!
- Purchase and use frozen ingredients, such as pepper stir-fry, corn, carrots, etc., to reduce prep time. These easy-to-measure ingredients help make healthier meals when energies are low.

FLAVOR FINDS

- Add a twist to a dish by reversing the marinade: Marinate with citrus or vinegar and oil, for example, by pouring it over the protein or veggies *after* they're cooked rather than before . . . the flavors will be more pronounced and there will be added moisture as well.
- Toast any nuts needed in a recipe before starting the recipe by cooking them for 3 to 4 minutes on Saute/Browning mode and set aside. This brings out the nuttiness without adding more calories or fat.
- Add a small amount, about 1 teaspoon, of instant coffee granules to give a dish a deeper, richer, "beefier" flavor.
- Squeeze a lemon or lime wedge over a dish just before serving to bring out the fresh taste of the other ingredients as well as the saltiness without adding more salt.
- After ingredients are cooked, remove them from the pot with a slotted spoon. Cancel and reset the cooker to Sauté/Browning. Bring the remaining liquid in the pot to a boil. Continue to boil until thickened slightly and deep flavors develop. Pour the liquid over the cooked items to enhance the flavors and provide moisture to the dish without adding more fat, calories, or sodium.

- When a "meatier" dish is desired in a meatless main, add sautéed mushrooms, in particular quartered mushrooms.
- A touch of honey doesn't add sweetness, but acts as a blender, providing overall mellowness to a dish.
- If you're cutting back on sugar when making your favorite desserts, reduce the overall amount by ¼ to ⅓ cup (50 to 67 g) and add an additional 1 teaspoon of vanilla. You won't miss the sugar because it isn't too drastic of a change, and the addition of vanilla enhances the overall sweetness of the sugar itself.
- Adding ½ teaspoon of grated orange or lemon zest or grated fresh ginger pulls the flavors up.

NUTRITION NUDGES

- Add more vitamin C to your dish simply by replacing a green bell pepper with a red bell pepper.
- Add more protein to your dish simply by replacing light sour cream with low-fat plain Greek yogurt.
- Brighten up your white rice using ground turmeric when cooking, which turns the rice a brilliant yellow color and makes the other ingredients pop!
- Multigrain pastas are lighter in texture and color than whole-wheat pastas but still provide a hefty amount of fiber and protein. Read the labels and look for pastas that are yellow rather than cream or tan in color.
- One clever way to sneak more nutrient-rich veggies into your dishes is by puréeing carrots or red bell peppers (or both) into spaghetti sauce and tomato-based soups. It enriches the overall color of the dish as well.
- Incorporate more fruits into your day by cooking fruits and topping with *one* cookie, crumbled, such as a vanilla wafer or a gingersnap, for a quick-fix crumble.

SANDWICHES AND WRAPS

When you think of sandwiches, the first thing that probably comes to mind is two pieces of bread with something in between—pretty boring, right? It's time to add some variety and brighten up the boring! Use tender lettuce leaves as cups to hold those sandwich fillings, make the most out of crusty French bread by getting the crunch without the carbs, and make "knife-and-fork" tortillas so you can stack ingredients high, really high. See? There's more to a sandwich than two pieces of bread!

SANDWICHES AND WRAPS

Hummus-Stuffed Tortilla Wraps 20

Pepper–Goat Cheese Toasts 21

Spiced Orange Chicken Bibb Wraps 23

Sweet-Hot Chicken Long-Leaf Wraps 25

Cheater's Barbecue Chicken 26

Lime'd Flank Tortillas with Guacamole 27

Shredded Brisket Po' Boys 28

So Sloppy Joes 30

Beef Hoagies 31

Lebanese Beef and Pecan–Stuffed Pitas 32

Tender Pork on Corn Tortillas with Avocado Mash 35

HUMMUS-STUFFED TORTILLA WRAPS

Here's a double recipe in one . . . use half the cooked hummus for your tortillas and reserve the remaining half for a healthy snack later with raw veggies . . . and the hummus freezes well, too.

4 cups (960 ml) water

1 cup (200 g) dried chickpeas, rinsed and drained

⅓ cup (53 g) chopped onion

2 garlic cloves, peeled

½ teaspoon dried rosemary

2 lemons

½ teaspoon ground cumin

½ teaspoon salt

1 tablespoon (15 ml) extra-virgin olive oil

4 high-fiber, low-carb wheat tortillas, warmed

4 cups (200 g) shredded romaine lettuce

1 cup (135 g) chopped cucumber

1 cup (180 g) chopped tomato

1 ounce (28 g) crumbled reduced-fat blue cheese or feta cheese

12 pitted Kalamata olives, coarsely chopped

In your pressure cooker cooking pot, combine the water, chickpeas, onion, garlic, and rosemary.

Lock the lid in place and close the seal valve. Press the Manual button to set the cook time for 45 minutes. When the cook time ends, use a natural pressure release for 10 minutes, then a quick pressure release.

When the valve drops, carefully remove the lid. Place a colander over a bowl and drain the chickpeas, reserving ¾ cup (180 ml) of the cooking liquid.

In a blender, combine the drained chickpea mixture, reserved cooking liquid, the juice of 1 lemon, the cumin, and salt. Secure the lid, holding it down firmly, and purée until smooth. Transfer to a bowl and stir in the olive oil.

Place the tortillas on a work surface. Spoon ¼ cup (56 g) of the puréed mixture down the center of each. Cut the remaining lemon into 4 wedges and squeeze 1 wedge over each tortilla. Top with equal amounts of lettuce, cucumber, tomato, cheese, and olives. Fold the sides over and cut the wrap in half.

Cover and refrigerate the remaining hummus for a healthy snack with raw veggies.

YIELD: Makes 2½ cups (560 g) hummus and 4 tortillas

SERVES 4: About ¼ cup (56 g) hummus, 1 tortilla, 1 cup (50 g) lettuce, ¼ cup (33.75 g) cucumber, ¼ cup (45 g) tomato, 1 tablespoon (7 g) cheese, and 3 olives per serving

Nutrition Facts

SERVING SIZE (182 G)

AMOUNT PER SERVING

Calories: 220

		% Daily Value
Total Fat	10g	13%
Saturated Fat	1g	5%
Trans Fat	0g	
Cholesterol	5mg	2%
Sodium	640mg	28%
Total Carbohydrate	29g	11%
Dietary Fiber	6g	21%
Total Sugars	5g	
Added Sugars	0g	
Protein	12g	
Vitamin D	0mcg	
Calcium	121g	10%
Iron	3mg	15%
Potassium	434mg	10%

PEPPER-GOAT CHEESE TOASTS

Toasts are very popular. These are piled high with brightly colored, oh-so-tender veggies, Greek olives, and garlic and sprinkled with goat cheese. Served with a knife and fork or enjoy out of hand.

12 garlic cloves, peeled

2 medium red bell peppers, coarsely chopped

2 medium green bell peppers, coarsely chopped

2 medium yellow squash, coarsely chopped

¾ cup (180 ml) water

12 pitted Kalamata olives, coarsely chopped

1 tablespoon (15 ml) extra-virgin olive oil

1 teaspoon dried oregano

1 teaspoon apple cider vinegar

½ teaspoon salt

8 ounces (225 g) multigrain baguette, cut into 12 slices

2 ounces (55 g) crumbled goat cheese

In your pressure cooker cooking pot, combine the garlic, red and green bell peppers, squash, and water.

Lock the lid in place and close the seal valve. Press the Manual button to set the cook time for 4 minutes. When the cook time ends, use a natural pressure release for 10 minutes, then a quick pressure release.

When the valve drops, carefully remove the lid. Using a slotted spoon, transfer the vegetables to a medium bowl. Stir in the olives, olive oil, oregano, vinegar, and salt to the bowl.

Divide the bread among 4 dinner plates. Top with the vegetables and sprinkle with the goat cheese.

YIELD: Makes 4 cups (900 g) vegetable mixture and 12 slices of toast

SERVES 4: 3 bread slices, 1 cup (225 g) vegetable mixture, and 2 tablespoons (14 g) goat cheese per serving

Nutrition Facts

SERVING SIZE (256 G)

AMOUNT PER SERVING

Calories: **300**

		% Daily Value
Total Fat	14g	18%
Saturated Fat	3g	15%
Trans Fat	0g	
Cholesterol	20mg	7%
Sodium	510mg	22%
Total Carbohydrate	37g	13%
Dietary Fiber	3g	11%
Total Sugars	8g	
Added Sugars	0g	
Protein	11g	
Vitamin D	0mcg	
Calcium	79mg	6%
Iron	2mg	10%
Potassium	360mg	8%

SPICED ORANGE CHICKEN BIBB WRAPS

It's important to let the cooked chicken rest for 10 minutes before chopping . . . it will go from tough to tender in just those few minutes . . . those very important few minutes!

2 tablespoons (16 g) sesame seeds

1 cup (240 ml) water

2 (8-ounce, or 225 g) frozen boneless, skinless chicken breasts

½ teaspoon smoked paprika

⅛ teaspoon salt

¼ teaspoon black pepper

FOR SAUCE:

¼ cup (60 ml) fresh orange juice

2½ tablespoons (50 g) honey

1 tablespoon (15 ml) canola oil

2 teaspoon Sriracha or other hot sauce

1½ teaspoons apple cider vinegar

⅛ teaspoon salt

¼ teaspoon grated orange zest

4 cups (340 g) coleslaw mix

½ cup (50 g) finely chopped scallions

12 large Bibb or Boston lettuce leaves

On your pressure cooker, select Sauté/Browning + more to preheat the cooking pot. Once hot, add the sesame seeds to the pot. Cook for 3 minutes, stirring occasionally. Transfer to a plate and set aside.

Place the water in the cooking pot. Add the chicken and sprinkle it with the paprika, salt, and pepper.

Lock the lid in place and close the seal valve. Press the Cancel button. Press the Manual button to set the cook time for 10 minutes. When the cook time ends, use a natural pressure release for 1 minute, then a quick pressure release.

When the valve drops, carefully remove the lid. Transfer the chicken to a cutting board and let rest for 10 minutes to cool. Chop the cooled chicken into bite-size pieces.

Meanwhile, make the sauce: In a small bowl, stir together the orange juice, honey, canola oil, Sriracha, vinegar, and salt.

(continued)

Nutrition Facts		
SERVING SIZE (230 G)		
AMOUNT PER SERVING		
Calories:	**250**	
		% Daily Value
Total Fat	9g	12%
Saturated Fat	1.5g	8%
Trans Fat	0g	
Cholesterol	60mg	20%
Sodium	270mg	12%
Total Carbohydrate	18g	7%
Dietary Fiber	2g	7%
Total Sugars	12g	
Added Sugars	10g	20%
Protein	24g	
Vitamin D	0mcg	0%
Calcium	64mg	4%
Iron	2mg	10%
Potassium	375mg	8%

Discard the liquid in the pot. Press the Cancel button. Select Sauté/Browning + more. Add the sauce to the pot. Bring to a boil. Cook for 1 minute, or until it reduces to ¼ cup (60 ml) of liquid, scraping up any browned bits from the bottom and sides of the pot. Pour the sauce back into the small bowl, stir in the orange zest, and let cool completely.

To serve, place equal amounts of the coleslaw, scallions, and chicken in each lettuce leaf. Spoon the sauce evenly over all and sprinkle with the toasted sesame seeds.

YIELD: Makes about 2 cups (340 g) cooked chicken, ¼ cup (60 ml) sauce, and 4 cups (340 g) coleslaw

SERVES 4: ½ cup (85 g) cooked chicken, 1 tablespoon (15 ml) sauce, and 1 cup (85 g) coleslaw per serving

SWEET-HOT CHICKEN LONG-LEAF WRAPS

A super speedy dish comes from freezer to pot with the added bonus of no chopping or trimming of the chicken . . . before or after! And these are fun to eat, too!

2 lemons

1 cup (240 ml) water, divided

8 frozen chicken tenderloins (about 1¼ pounds, or 569 g, total)

1 tablespoon (15 ml) Sriracha

⅓ cup (75 g) light mayonnaise

1½ tablespoons (30 g) honey

1½ teaspoons prepared yellow mustard

8 large romaine lettuce leaves

4 cups (200 g) shredded romaine lettuce

1 avocado, peeled, pitted, and chopped

½ cup (8 g) chopped fresh cilantro

⅛ teaspoon salt

Slice 1 lemon and place it into your pressure cooker cooking pot. Add all but 1 tablespoon (15 ml) of the water. Arrange the chicken on top of the lemon slices and brush the Sriracha evenly over the chicken.

Lock the lid in place and close the seal valve. Press the Manual button to set the cook time for 2 minutes. When the cook time ends, use a natural pressure release for 5 minutes, then a quick pressure release.

When the valve drops, carefully remove the lid. Transfer the chicken to a plate and let cool for 5 minutes.

Meanwhile, in a small bowl, stir together the mayonnaise, honey, mustard, and reserved 1 tablespoon (15 ml) of water.

Place the romaine lettuce leaves on a work surface. Top each with equal amounts of shredded lettuce. Squeeze the juice of the remaining lemon evenly over all. Top each with 1 chicken tender and drizzle with the mayonnaise sauce.

Divide the avocado among the wraps. Sprinkle with cilantro and season with salt.

YIELD: Makes 12 ounces (336 g) cooked chicken, 4 cups (200 g) lettuce, 1 avocado and about 1/2 cup (120 g) sauce

SERVES 4: 3 ounces (84 g) cooked chicken, 1 cup (50 g) lettuce, ¼ avocado, and about 2 tablespoons (30 g) sauce per serving

Nutrition Facts

SERVING SIZE (324 G)

AMOUNT PER SERVING

Calories: **270**

		% Daily Value
Total Fat	11g	14%
Saturated Fat	1.5g	8%
Trans Fat	0g	
Cholesterol	60mg	20%
Sodium	450mg	20%
Total Carbohydrate	17g	6%
Dietary Fiber	3g	11%
Total Sugars	8g	
Added Sugars	6g	12%
Protein	29g	
Vitamin D	0mcg	
Calcium	45mg	4%
Iron	2mg	10%
Potassium	320mg	6%

CHEATER'S BARBECUE CHICKEN

Here's a perfect weeknight barbecue. It's great to keep all the ingredients on hand for a quick meal, and you can serve it on buns, in baked potatoes, and even wrapped in long lettuce leaves!

2¼ pounds (1 kg) boneless, skinless chicken thighs, trimmed of fat

1 cup (160 g) chopped onion

¾ cup (180 ml) water

2 tablespoons (30 ml) balsamic vinegar

2 teaspoons Worcestershire sauce

1 teaspoon smoked paprika

⅛ teaspoon cayenne pepper

⅔ cup (170 g) barbecue sauce, divided

⅛ teaspoon salt (optional)

8 whole-wheat hamburger buns

In your pressure cooker cooking pot, combine the chicken, onion, water, vinegar, Worcestershire sauce, paprika, cayenne, and all but 2 tablespoons (32 g) of the barbecue sauce.

Lock the lid in place and close the seal valve. Press the Manual button to set the cook time for 15 minutes. When the cook time ends, use a quick pressure release.

When the valve drops, carefully remove the lid. Transfer the chicken to a cutting board and let it rest for 5 minutes before coarsely shredding it.

Place a colander over a bowl and strain the liquid from the pot, reserving ½ (120 ml) cup of cooking liquid and the strained onions.

Press the Cancel button. Select Sauté/Browning + more. Return the shredded chicken, the reserved cooking liquid, strained onions, and salt (if using) to the pot. Bring to a boil. Cook for 4 minutes, or until thickened, stirring occasionally.

Wearing oven mitts, remove the pot from the pressure cooker and place it on a heatproof surface. Stir in the remaining 2 tablespoons (32 g) of barbecue sauce. Serve with the buns.

YIELD: Makes about 4 cups (900 g) chicken mixture and 8 buns

SERVES 8: About ½ cup (112 g) chicken mixture and 1 bun per serving

Nutrition Facts

SERVING SIZE (155 G)

AMOUNT PER SERVING

Calories: **340**

		% Daily Value
Total Fat	6g	8%
Saturated Fat	1.5g	8%
Trans Fat	0g	
Cholesterol	100mg	33%
Sodium	580mg	25%
Total Carbohydrate	36g	13%
Dietary Fiber	0g	
Total Sugars	13g	
Added Sugars	0g	
Protein	26g	
Vitamin D	0mcg	
Calcium	106mg	8%
Iron	3mg	15%
Potassium	41mg	0%

LIME'D FLANK TORTILLAS WITH GUACAMOLE

The beef in this dish is cooked with lime juice, Worcestershire sauce, smoked paprika, and cumin. Then the liquid is cooked down to a rich thick paste and spread over the cooked beef, which is sliced and served over tortillas with guac and tomatoes . . . words cannot describe how delicious it is!

⅔ cup (160 ml) water

3 limes

1 tablespoon (15 ml) Worcestershire sauce

2 teaspoons smoked paprika

1 teaspoon ground cumin

1 teaspoon Monterey steak grilling blend

1 pound (454 g) flank steak

4 high-fiber, low-carb tortillas

1 (8-ounce, or 225 g) container prepared guacamole

1 cup (180 g) chopped tomatoes

In your pressure cooker cooking pot, combine the water, the juice of 2 limes, and the Worcestershire sauce.

In a small bowl, stir together the paprika, cumin, and grilling blend. Sprinkle the spices over both sides of the steak, pressing with your fingertips to adhere. Place the beef in the pot.

Lock the lid in place and close the seal valve. Press the Manual button to set the cook time for 12 minutes. When the cook time ends, use a quick pressure release.

When the valve drops, carefully remove the lid. Press the Cancel button. Select Sauté/Browning + more. Bring the mixture to a boil. Cook, uncovered, for 12 minutes, or until the liquid is almost evaporated. (Note: It will appear to be a loose paste at this stage).

Transfer the beef to a cutting board, spoon the paste over the beef, and let stand for 5 minutes before thinly slicing.

Warm the tortillas according to the package directions.

Cut the remaining lime into 4 wedges. Spoon equal amounts of guacamole down the center of each tortilla. Top with the beef and tomatoes. Squeeze lime juice over all, fold the edges over, and halve, if desired.

YIELD: Makes 12 ounces (340 g) cooked beef, 1 cup (224) guacamole, 1 cup (180 g) tomatoes

SERVES 4: 1 tortilla (36 g), 3 ounces (85 g) cooked beef, ¼ cup (56 g) guacamole, and ¼ cup (45 g) chopped tomatoes per serving

Nutrition Facts

SERVING SIZE (222 G)

AMOUNT PER SERVING

Calories: 320

		% Daily Value
Total Fat	17g	22%
Saturated Fat	4g	20%
Trans Fat	0g	
Cholesterol	70mg	23%
Sodium	520mg	23%
Total Carbohydrate	13g	5%
Dietary Fiber	1g	4%
Total Sugars	1g	
Added Sugars	0g	
Protein	31g	
Vitamin D	0mcg	
Calcium	74mg	6%
Iron	3mg	15%
Potassium	510mg	10%

SHREDDED BRISKET PO' BOYS

When cutting back on calories, it can sometimes be difficult to include sandwiches made with French or Italian bread. Here's a way to get the bread you want and stay on track, too.

Nonstick cooking spray, for preparing the cooking pot

1½ pounds (679 g) lean flat-cut beef brisket, trimmed of fat, patted dry with paper towels

1 cup (160 g) chopped onion

¾ cup (180 ml) dry red wine

¼ cup (60 ml) water

2 teaspoons balsamic vinegar

5 garlic cloves, peeled

1 tablespoon (6 g) sodium-free beef bouillon granules

2 teaspoons instant coffee granules

1½ teaspoons sugar

1 teaspoon dried thyme

2 bay leaves

2 (8-ounce, or 225 g) loaves whole-grain Italian bread, halved lengthwise

¾ teaspoon salt

On your pressure cooker, select Sauté/Browning + more to preheat the cooking pot. Once hot, coat the pot with cooking spray. Add the beef. Cook for 3 minutes on one side. Turn the beef and top with the onion, red wine, water, vinegar, garlic, bouillon granules, coffee granules, sugar, thyme, and bay leaves.

Lock the lid in place and close the seal valve. Press the Cancel button. Press the Manual button to set the cook time for 1 hour, 15 minutes. When the cook time ends, use a natural pressure release.

When the valve drops, carefully remove the lid. Transfer the beef to a cutting board and let stand for 10 minutes before shredding.

Meanwhile, remove the center portion of the bread halves, leaving a ½-inch (1 cm) border. The bread should weigh 12 ounces (340 g) after removing the center portion. Arrange the bread "shells" on a baking sheet and place them into a cold oven. Set the oven to 325°F (170°C)—there's no need to preheat—and bake for 8 minutes to crisp slightly. Remove from the oven and let cool. (The bread will become slightly firm once cool.)

Nutrition Facts

SERVING SIZE (184 G)

AMOUNT PER SERVING

Calories: **330**

		% Daily Value
Total Fat	8g	10%
Saturated Fat	2g	10%
Trans Fat	0g	
Cholesterol	70mg	23%
Sodium	580mg	25%
Total Carbohydrate	30g	11%
Dietary Fiber	1g	4%
Total Sugars	6g	
Added Sugars	1g	2%
Protein	30g	
Vitamin D	0mcg	
Calcium	57mg	4%
Iron	3mg	15%
Potassium	269mg	6%

Press the Cancel button. Select Sauté/Browning + more. Bring the liquid in the pot to a boil. Cook, uncovered, for 10 minutes, or until thickened slightly. Remove and discard the bay leaves.

Add the shredded beef and salt to the pot. Cook for 5 minutes to let the flavors blend. Spoon equal amounts onto the bottom of each bread shell. Top with some pan juices and the remaining bread shell halves, pressing down gently.

YIELD: Makes 3 cups (510 g) beef mixture, ¾ cup (180 ml) pan juices, and 12 ounces (340 g) bread

SERVES 6: ½ cup (168 g) beef mixture, 2 tablespoons (30 ml) pan juices, and 2 ounces (55 g) bread per serving

SO SLOPPY JOES

Most of us think of toasting buns in an oven or preheating a broiler, but all you have to do is pop them in your toaster! That saves time and energy and keeps the kitchen cool!

Nonstick cooking spray, for preparing the cooking pot

1 pound (454 g) lean ground beef

2 cups (270 g) frozen mixed vegetables

1 cup (150 g) chopped green bell pepper

½ cup (120 ml) water

1½ tablespoons (23 ml) Worcestershire sauce

1 tablespoon (15 ml) balsamic vinegar

2 teaspoons ground cumin

1 teaspoon smoked paprika

½ cup (130 g) tomato paste

2 teaspoons sugar

¾ teaspoon salt

8 whole-wheat hamburger buns, toasted

On your pressure cooker, select Sauté/Browning + more to preheat the cooking pot. Once hot, coat the pot with cooking spray. Add the ground beef. Cook for about 3 minutes until no longer pink, stirring occasionally. Add the frozen vegetables, green bell pepper, water, Worcestershire sauce, vinegar, cumin, and paprika. Spoon the tomato paste on top and sprinkle evenly with the sugar. *Do not stir.*

Lock the lid in place and close the seal valve. Press the Cancel button. Press the Manual button to set the cook time for 5 minutes. When the cook time ends, use a quick pressure release.

When the valve drops, carefully remove the lid. Stir in the salt. Serve over the hamburger buns.

YIELD: Makes 4 cups (1 kg) beef mixture and 8 buns

SERVES 8: ½ cup (125 g) beef mixture and 1 bun per serving

Nutrition Facts

SERVING SIZE (174 G)

AMOUNT PER SERVING

Calories: **280**

		% Daily Value
Total Fat	7g	9%
Saturated Fat	2.5g	13%
Trans Fat	0g	
Cholesterol	35mg	12%
Sodium	660mg	29%
Total Carbohydrate	36g	13%
Dietary Fiber	0g	
Total Sugars	9g	
Added Sugars	1g	2%
Protein	20g	
Vitamin D	0mcg	
Calcium	130mg	10%
Iron	2mg	10%
Potassium	356mg	8%

BEEF HOAGIES

You can purchase sliced peperoncini in the olive and pickle aisle of major supermarkets, but if you only find whole, just slice them into thin rounds. Don't substitute another pepper; they add personality and punch to the hoagies.

Nonstick cooking spray, for preparing the cooking pot

2 red bell peppers (or 1 red pepper and 1 yellow pepper), thinly sliced

⅓ cup (40 g) sliced peperoncini

2 pounds (908 g) lean boneless chuck roast, cut into 4 to 6 pieces, trimmed of fat

½ cup (120 ml) red wine

⅓ cup (80 ml) water

1 tablespoon (15 ml) Worcestershire sauce

2 teaspoons dried Italian seasoning

1 teaspoon garlic powder

¾ teaspoon salt

½ teaspoon black pepper

8 (2-ounce, or 56 g) hoagie rolls

On your pressure cooker, select Sauté/Browning + more to preheat the cooking pot. Once hot, coat the pot with cooking spray. Add the bell peppers. Cook for 8 minutes, or until lightly browned on the edges, stirring occasionally. Stir in the peperoncini. Cook for 15 seconds. Transfer the pepper mixture to a plate and set aside.

Coat the pot again with cooking spray. Add half the beef. Cook *without turning* for 5 minutes. Turn the beef and add the red wine, water, Worcestershire sauce, Italian seasoning, garlic powder, salt, and pepper.

Lock the lid in place and close the seal valve. Press the Cancel button. Press the Manual button to set the cook time for 40 minutes. When the cook time ends, use a natural pressure release.

When the valve drops, carefully remove the lid. Remove the beef from the pot and coarsely shred it. Turn off the pressure cooker. Pour the pan juices into a fat separator. (Alternatively, place the liquid in a resealable freezer bag. Let the fat rise to the top. Hold the bag over a 2-cup [480 ml] measuring cup, snip one end of the bag, and let the pan juices flow into the measuring cup. Stop the flow when it comes close to the fat.) Discard the fat and return the pan juices to the pressure cooker pot.

Place equal amounts of beef on each roll. Top with the pepper mixture and serve with the dipping sauce.

YIELD: Makes 4 cups (595 g) cooked beef, 2 cups (255 g) pepper mixture, 1 cup (240 ml) dipping sauce, and 8 rolls

SERVES 8: ½ cup (74 g) beef, about ¼ cup (32 g) pepper mixture, 2 tablespoons (30 ml) dipping sauce, and 1 roll per serving

Nutrition Facts

SERVING SIZE (176 G)

AMOUNT PER SERVING

Calories: 350

		% Daily Value
Total Fat	12g	15%
Saturated Fat	3.5g	18%
Trans Fat	0g	
Cholesterol	60mg	20%
Sodium	630mg	27%
Total Carbohydrate	30g	11%
Dietary Fiber	1g	4%
Total Sugars	4g	
Added Sugars	0g	
Protein	26g	
Vitamin D	0mcg	
Calcium	82mg	6%
Iron	3mg	15%
Potassium	242mg	6%

LEBANESE BEEF AND PECAN-STUFFED PITAS

Take a break from spaghetti or tacos and enjoy this unique and scrumptious way to use that pound of frozen ground beef in your freezer. Serve it in pita pockets, on hamburger buns, or over 2 cups cooked rice.

2 ounces (55 g) chopped pecans

1 cup (240 ml) water

1 cup (160 g) chopped onion

½ teaspoon ground cinnamon

½ teaspoon ground cumin

¼ teaspoon ground allspice

⅛ teaspoon red pepper flakes

1 pound (454 g) frozen extra-lean ground beef

1 tablespoon (15 g) ketchup

½ teaspoon salt

⅛ teaspoon black pepper

2 white or whole-wheat pita rounds (about 6 inches, or 15 cm), halved and warmed

¼ cup (60 g) plain 2% Greek yogurt

On your pressure cooker cooking pot, select Sauté/Browning + more to preheat the cooking pot. Once hot, add the pecans to the pot. Cook for 4 minutes, stirring occasionally. Remove and set aside. Add the water to the cooking pot. Stir in the onion, cinnamon, cumin, allspice, and red pepper flakes. Add the frozen ground beef.

Lock the lid in place and close the seal valve. Press the Cancel button. Press the Manual button to set the cook time for 5 minutes. When the cook time ends, use a quick pressure release.

When the valve drops, carefully remove the lid. Press the Cancel button. Select Sauté/Browning + more. Stir in the ketchup, salt, black pepper, and pecans. Cook for 8 to 10 minutes, or until the liquid is almost evaporated, stirring to break up larger pieces of beef while cooking (some liquid should still remain).

Spoon equal amounts of the beef mixture into each pita half. Top each with 1 tablespoon (15 g) of yogurt.

YIELD: Makes 3 cups (1 pound, 14 ounces or 848 grams) beef mixture

SERVES 4: ¾ cup (212 g) beef mixture, ½ pita round, and 1 tablespoon (15 g) yogurt

Nutrition Facts		
SERVING SIZE (212 G)		
AMOUNT PER SERVING		
Calories:	**320**	
		% Daily Value
Total Fat	14g	18%
Saturated Fat	4.5g	23%
Trans Fat	0g	
Cholesterol	70mg	23%
Sodium	580mg	25%
Total Carbohydrate	24g	9%
Dietary Fiber	1g	4%
Total Sugars	4g	
Added Sugars	1g	2%
Protein	29g	
Vitamin D	0mcg	
Calcium	34mg	2%
Iron	1mg	6%
Potassium	154mg	4%

TENDER PORK ON CORN TORTILLAS WITH AVOCADO MASH

Bite into an explosion of taste and texture. Warm corn tortillas topped with garlic and lime avocado, tender pork, juicy peppers, and crisp romaine . . . perfection!

1 pound (454 g) boneless pork shoulder, trimmed of fat, cut into 1-inch (2.5 cm) cubes

1 teaspoon smoked paprika

1½ teaspoons ground cumin

Nonstick cooking spray, for preparing the cooking pot

1 teaspoon canola oil

2 poblano peppers, seeded and cut into thin strips

1 cup (240 ml) water

1 avocado, halved and pitted

1 garlic clove, minced

½ teaspoon salt, divided

2 tablespoons (30 ml) fresh lemon juice

¼ teaspoon black pepper

8 corn tortillas, warmed

4 cups (200 g) shredded romaine lettuce

1 lemon, quartered

Season the pork with the paprika and cumin. On your pressure cooker, select Sauté/Browning + more to preheat the cooking pot. Once hot, coat the pot with cooking spray. Add the canola oil and tilt the pot to coat the bottom lightly. Add the seasoned pork in a single layer. Cook for 5 minutes, *without stirring*. Stir in the poblanos and water, scraping up any browned bits from the bottom of the pot.

Lock the lid in place and close the seal valve. Press the Cancel button. Press the Manual button to set the cook time for 20 minutes. When the cook time ends, use a quick pressure release.

Meanwhile, in a bowl combine the avocado, the garlic, and ¼ teaspoon of salt. Mash well. Stir in the lemon juice until well blended. Set aside.

When the valve drops, carefully remove the lid. With a slotted spoon, transfer the pork and peppers to a shallow pan or bowl. Sprinkle with the remaining ¼ teaspoon of salt and the black pepper. Toss gently.

Top each warm tortilla with equal amounts of the avocado mixture, shredded romaine, and pork mixture. Squeeze lemon juice evenly over all and fold the ends over.

YIELD: Makes 2 cups (336 g) cooked pork, 4 cups (200 g) romaine lettuce, ½ cup (115 g) avocado mash, and 8 tortillas

SERVES 4: ½ cup (84 g) cooked pork, 1 cup (50 g) lettuce, 2 tablespoons (29 g) avocado mash, and 2 tortillas per serving

Nutrition Facts

SERVING SIZE (196 G)

AMOUNT PER SERVING

Calories: 320

		% Daily Value
Total Fat	15g	19%
Saturated Fat	3.5g	18%
Trans Fat	0g	
Cholesterol	70mg	23%
Sodium	580mg	25%
Total Carbohydrate	21g	8%
Dietary Fiber	4g	14%
Total Sugars	4g	
Added Sugars	0g	
Protein	25g	
Vitamin D	1mcg	6%
Calcium	65mg	6%
Iron	3mg	15%

MAIN-COURSE SALADS

Salads . . . in a pressure cooker? Really? Why?
Because you can broaden your salad choices and salad
ingredients by being able to transform frozen, hard-as-a-
rock chicken or salmon into tender, "salad-ready"
ingredients in a fraction of the time. You can cook lentils
and dried beans in a *flash*! You can even make
hardboiled eggs with shells that literally slip off . . . no bits
of shell stuck to the eggs ever again! You can also
double up the items you're pressure cooking to keep extra
(chicken, fish, lentils, or eggs) on hand for another
use later in the week. That helps to simplify meal prep, too!
That's why the pressure cooker is such a great tool!

MAIN-COURSE SALADS

Fresh Cucumber, Feta, and Lentil Salad 40

Deviled Egg Salad on Spring Greens 41

Fiesta Bright Rice Salad 42

Layered Egg and Fresh Crouton Salad Bowls 44

Curried Chicken Salad on Melon 47

Fresh Lemon-Ginger Salmon Salad 48

Tomato-Peperoncini Rotini Salad 49

Lemon-Mint Chicken Couscous Salad 50

Farro Salad with Salami, Kale, and Olive 52

Ham and Potato Salad with Dill 53

FRESH CUCUMBER, FETA, AND LENTIL SALAD

Incorporate more fiber and protein into your meals by replacing pasta with lentils. This meatless main salad serves up 6 grams of fiber and 14 grams of protein while keeping the carbs under control.

¾ cup (144 g) dried green or brown lentils, rinsed

2 cups (480 ml) water

1 cup (135 g) chopped cucumber

1 cup (149 g) grape tomatoes, quartered

4 ounces (115 g) crumbled reduced-fat feta cheese

½ cup (32 g) chopped fresh mint

¼ cup (40 g) finely chopped red onion

¼ cup (15 g) chopped fresh parsley

3 tablespoons (45 ml) red wine vinegar

2 tablespoons (30 ml) extra-virgin olive oil

½ teaspoon salt

⅛ teaspoon to ¼ teaspoon red pepper flakes

In your pressure cooker cooking pot, combine the lentils and water.

Lock the lid in place and close the seal valve. Press the Manual button to set the cook time for 7 minutes. When the cook time ends, use a quick pressure release.

When the valve drops, carefully remove the lid. Transfer the lentils to a colander to drain and run under cold water to stop the cooking and cool them quickly.

Meanwhile, in a medium bowl, combine the remaining ingredients and stir to combine. Add the cooled lentils and toss until well blended. Cover and refrigerate for 1 hour before serving.

YIELD: Makes 5 cups (616 g) salad

SERVES 4: 1¼ cups (231 g) per serving

Nutrition Facts

SERVING SIZE (154 G)

AMOUNT PER SERVING

Calories: 270

		% Daily Value
Total Fat	11g	14%
Saturated Fat	3g	15%
Trans Fat	0g	
Cholesterol	10mg	3%
Sodium	650mg	28%
Total Carbohydrate	25g	9%
Dietary Fiber	6g	21%
Total Sugars	3g	
Added Sugars	0g	
Protein	14g	
Vitamin D	0mcg	
Calcium	102mg	8%
Iron	3mg	15%
Potassium	488mg	10%

DEVILED EGG SALAD ON SPRING GREENS

You will never again have to pick off bits and pieces of shell from your hardboiled eggs. Smooth, large pieces of eggshell will slip off *soooo* easily . . . see for yourself!

1 cup (240 ml) water

6 large eggs

¼ cup (60 g) light mayonnaise

1 tablespoon (11 g) prepared yellow mustard

1 tablespoon (15 ml) apple cider vinegar

1 teaspoon sugar

¼ teaspoon salt

⅛ teaspoon cayenne pepper

1 cup (100 g) chopped celery

4 cups spring greens (284 g) or microgreens (100 g)

1 avocado, peeled, pitted, and sliced

Put a trivet into your pressure cooker cooking pot and pour in the water. Place the eggs on the trivet.

Lock the lid in place and close the seal valve. Press the Manual button to set the cook time for 7 minutes. Make an ice bath by placing 2 cups (240 g) of ice cubes in a bowl with 2 cups (480 ml) of water and place near the pressure cooker. When the cook time ends, use a quick pressure release.

When the valve drops, carefully remove the lid. Immediately transfer the eggs into the bowl of ice water. Let stand in the water for 3 minutes.

Meanwhile, in a medium bowl, whisk the mayonnaise, mustard, vinegar, sugar, salt, and cayenne until well blended.

Peel and chop the eggs. Add to the mayonnaise mixture along with the celery. Gently stir until well blended. Serve over the spring greens topped with avocado slices.

YIELD: Makes 3 cups (213 g) egg salad, 4 cups (284 g) spring greens, and 1 cup (146 g) avocado total

SERVES 4: ¾ cup egg mixture, 1 cup (71 g) spring greens, and ¼ cup (36.5 g) avocado per serving

Nutrition Facts

SERVING SIZE (196 G)

AMOUNT PER SERVING

Calories: **220**

		% Daily Value
Total Fat	16g	21%
Saturated Fat	3.5g	18%
Trans Fat	0g	
Cholesterol	285mg	95%
Sodium	480mg	21%
Total Carbohydrate	8g	3%
Dietary Fiber	4g	14%
Total Sugars	2g	
Added Sugars	1g	2%
Protein	11g	
Vitamin D	2mcg	10%
Calcium	89mg	6%
Iron	3mg	15%
Potassium	347mg	8%

FIESTA BRIGHT RICE SALAD

Brighten up your salad using ground turmeric when cooking the white rice.
The turmeric turns the rice brilliant yellow and makes the other ingredients pop!

1¼ cups (300 ml) water

1 cup (185 g) uncooked long-grain white rice, rinsed

1 jalapeño pepper, seeded and finely chopped

¼ teaspoon ground turmeric

1½ cups (270 g) chopped tomato

1 avocado, peeled, pitted, and chopped

½ cup (50 g) chopped celery

¼ cup (40 g) chopped red onion

2 tablespoons (30 ml) apple cider vinegar

2 teaspoons extra-virgin olive oil

1 teaspoon salt

½ teaspoon ground cumin

2 ounces (55 g) shredded reduced-fat Mexican cheese blend or sharp white Cheddar cheese

¼ cup (4 g) chopped fresh cilantro (optional)

In your pressure cooker cooking pot, combine the water, rice, jalapeño, and turmeric.

Lock the lid in place and close the seal valve. Press the Manual button to set the cook time for 4 minutes. When the cook time ends, use a natural pressure release for 10 minutes, then a quick pressure release.

When the valve drops, carefully remove the lid. Transfer the cooked rice onto a sheet of aluminum foil or a baking sheet in a thin layer. Let stand for 10 minutes to cool completely.

Meanwhile, in a large bowl combine the tomato, avocado, celery, red onion, vinegar, olive oil, salt, and cumin. Gently stir to combine. Add the cooled rice, cheese, and cilantro (if using). Gently toss until blended.

YIELD: Makes 5 cups (1.2 kg) salad

SERVES 4: 1¼ cups (296 g) per serving

Nutrition Facts

SERVING SIZE (296 G)

AMOUNT PER SERVING

Calories: **330**

		% Daily Value
Total Fat	12g	15%
Saturated Fat	3.5g	18%
Trans Fat	0g	
Cholesterol	15mg	5%
Sodium	650mg	28%
Total Carbohydrate	48g	17%
Dietary Fiber	4g	14%
Total Sugars	3g	
Added Sugars	0g	
Protein	9g	
Vitamin D	0mcg	
Calcium	128mg	10%
Iron	2mg	10%
Potassium	459mg	10%

LAYERED EGG AND FRESH CROUTON SALAD BOWLS

This will become one of your favorite salads . . . *ever*. Besides the fact that the peelings literally slip off the cooked eggs, the croutons add another dimension of flavor and crunch . . . and it's made all in one pot! Make more croutons and store them in an airtight container to have on hand, if you like!

1 tablespoon (15 ml) canola oil

2 ounces (55 g) multigrain Italian bread, cut into ½-inch (1 cm) slices, then into ½-inch (1 cm) cubes

1½ teaspoons dried dill, divided

2 cups (480 ml) water

6 large eggs

8 cups (384 g) torn romaine lettuce

¾ cup (180 g) ranch-style yogurt dressing

⅛ teaspoon black pepper

½ cup (80 g) finely chopped red onion

½ cup (65 g) frozen green peas, thawed (see Cook's Note)

⅛ teaspoon salt

On your pressure cooker, select Sauté/Browning + more to preheat the cooking pot. Once hot, add the canola oil to the pot and tilt the pot to coat the bottom lightly. Add the bread cubes in a single layer. Cook for 2 minutes, *without stirring*. Sprinkle with ½ teaspoon dill. Cook for 4 minutes more, stirring occasionally, until they begin to brown. (All sides may not brown evenly.) Transfer to a plate and set aside. Let cool completely to become crisp.

Add the water to the pressure cooker cooking pot and place the steamer basket inside the pot. Place the eggs in the steamer basket.

Lock the lid in place and close the seal valve. Press the Cancel button. Press the Manual button to set the cook time for 7 minutes. When the cook time ends, use a quick pressure release.

Meanwhile, prepare an ice bath in a medium bowl and set aside (see Cook's Note on page 45).

When the valve drops, carefully remove the lid. Using tongs or a large spoon, immediately transfer the eggs to the ice water. Let stand for 3 minutes. Peel and slice the eggs.

Nutrition Facts

SERVING SIZE (269 G)

AMOUNT PER SERVING

Calories: **260**

		% Daily Value
Total Fat	16g	21%
Saturated Fat	3.5g	18%
Trans Fat	0g	
Cholesterol	285mg	95%
Sodium	660mg	29%
Total Carbohydrate	17g	6%
Dietary Fiber	2g	7%
Total Sugars	6g	
Added Sugars	0g	
Protein	14g	
Vitamin D	2mcg	10%
Calcium	123mg	10%
Iron	3mg	15%
Potassium	365mg	8%

Arrange an equal amount of romaine lettuce in each of 4 shallow bowls. Top with equal amounts of the egg slices, covering the entire surface of the lettuce bowl. Drizzle evenly with the ranch dressing. Sprinkle the salads with remaining 1 teaspoon of dill and the pepper. Top each with 2 tablespoons (20 g) of the red onion and 2 tablespoons (16.25 g) of the green peas. Top with the croutons and sprinkle with the salt.

YIELD: Makes about 10 cups (829 g) salad, ¾ cup (180 g) dressing, and 1⅓ cups (68 g) croutons

SERVES 4: About 2½ cups (207 g) salad, 3 tablespoons (45 g) dressing, plus ⅓ cup (17 g) croutons per serving

---

Cook's Note

Combine about 2 cups (280 g) ice cubes with 4 cups (960 ml) water to make an ice bath. To thaw frozen peas quickly, place them in a colander and run under cold water for 30 seconds. Drain well.

CURRIED CHICKEN SALAD ON MELON

Toasting nuts is important to bring out the nuttiness without overdoing the fat and calories, but they can burn quickly if you don't pay attention. Following is an easy way to toast them and not worry about the burning.

1 ounce (28 g) slivered almonds

12 ounces (340 g) frozen boneless, skinless chicken breasts

1 cup (240 ml) water

1½ teaspoons curry powder, divided

1 (8-ounce, or 225 g) can sliced water chestnuts, drained and chopped

½ cup (75 g) raisins, preferably golden

¼ cup (60 g) light mayonnaise

2 tablespoons (30 ml) fresh lemon juice

2 tablespoons (20 g) finely chopped red onion

¼ teaspoon ground cumin

¼ teaspoon salt

Pinch cayenne pepper

1 small cantaloupe, peeled, seeded, and cut into 8 wedges

On your pressure cooker, select Sauté/Browning + more to preheat the cooking pot. Once hot, add the almonds to the pot. Cook for 4 minutes, stirring occasionally, until fragrant or just beginning to lightly brown. Transfer to a plate and set aside.

In the pot, combine the chicken and water. Sprinkle with ½ teaspoon of curry powder.

Lock the lid in place and close the seal valve. Press the Cancel button. Press the Manual button to set the cook time for 10 minutes. When the cook time ends, use a natural pressure release for 2 minutes, then a quick pressure release.

When the valve drops, carefully remove the lid. Place the chicken on a cutting board. Let rest for 3 to 5 minutes before chopping. Discard the liquid in the pot.

In a medium bowl, stir together the water chestnuts, raisins, mayonnaise, lemon juice, red onion, cumin, salt, cayenne, and remaining 1 teaspoon of curry powder. Add the chicken. Stir until well coated in the dressing. Cover and refrigerate for 1 hour to let the flavors absorb and for the curry to turn a soft yellow color.

Serve the salad with the melon slices.

YIELD: Makes 4 cups (384 g) chicken salad plus 1 melon

SERVES 4: 1 cup (96 g) chicken salad plus 2 melon wedges per serving

Nutrition Facts

SERVING SIZE (275 G)

AMOUNT PER SERVING

Calories: 310

		% Daily Value
Total Fat	11g	14%
Saturated Fat	1g	5%
Trans Fat	0g	
Cholesterol	65mg	22%
Sodium	340mg	15%
Total Carbohydrate	31g	11%
Dietary Fiber	2g	7%
Total Sugars	22g	
Added Sugars	0g	
Protein	23g	
Vitamin D	0mcg	
Calcium	48mg	4%
Iron	2mg	10%
Potassium	837mg	20%

FRESH LEMON-GINGER SALMON SALAD

The salmon is quickly cooked, flaked, and served over a bed of delicate greens with avocado and jalapeño. Topped with a splash of fresh ginger, fresh lemon, and a bit of sweetness . . . perfect for those hot-weather nights (or days!).

FOR SALAD:

1 cup (240 ml) water

2 (6-ounce, or 170 g) frozen salmon fillets

½ lemon

¼ teaspoon black pepper

6 cups (426 g) spring greens

1 avocado, peeled, pitted, and chopped

¼ cup (40 g) finely chopped red onion

1 jalapeño pepper, halved lengthwise, seeded, and thinly sliced

FOR DRESSING:

2 tablespoons (25 g) sugar

2 teaspoons grated lemon zest

¼ cup (60 ml) fresh lemon juice

2 tablespoons (30 ml) canola oil

1 tablespoon (8 g) grated peeled fresh ginger

½ teaspoon salt

TO MAKE THE SALAD: Add the water to the pressure cooker cooking pot and place the steamer basket inside the pot. Place the salmon in the steamer basket. Squeeze the lemon half over the fish and sprinkle with the black pepper.

Lock the lid in place and close the seal valve. Press the Manual button to set the cook time for 4 minutes. When the cook time ends, use a quick pressure release.

When the valve drops, carefully remove the lid. Transfer the salmon to a plate and let cool for about 15 minutes.

Arrange equal amounts of spring greens on each of 4 dinner plates. Flake the salmon and place equal amounts on top of each salad. Top each with ¼ of the avocado, 1 tablespoon (10 g) of red onion, and ¼ of the jalapeño.

TO MAKE THE DRESSING: In a small bowl, whisk the dressing ingredients until well blended. Spoon 2 tablespoons (30 ml) over each salad.

YIELD: Makes 8 cups (700 g) salad plus ½ cup (120 ml) dressing

SERVES 4: 2 cups salad (225 g) plus 2 tablespoons (30 ml) dressing per serving

Nutrition Facts

SERVING SIZE (235 G)

AMOUNT PER SERVING

Calories: 280

		% Daily Value
Total Fat	17g	22%
Saturated Fat	2g	10%
Trans Fat	0g	
Cholesterol	45mg	15%
Sodium	390mg	17%
Total Carbohydrate	15g	5%
Dietary Fiber	4g	14%
Total Sugars	7g	
Added Sugars	6g	12%
Protein	20g	
Vitamin D	0mcg	
Calcium	63mg	4%
Iron	3mg	15%
Potassium	211mg	4%

TOMATO-PEPERONCINI ROTINI SALAD

Multigrain pastas are lighter in texture and color than whole-wheat pastas
but provide a hefty amount of fiber and protein. Read the front labels and look for pastas that are
yellow rather than cream or tan in color.

2 cups (480 ml) water, plus more as needed

3 ounces (85 g) multigrain rotini pasta (such as Barilla Plus)

1 (15.5-ounce, or 439 g) can no-salt-added chickpeas, rinsed and drained

1 pint (340 g) grape tomatoes, halved

1 (14-ounce, or 397 g) can quartered artichoke hearts, drained

3 ounces (¾ cup, or 85 g) sliced peperoncini

½ cup (80 g) chopped red onion

¼ cup (10 g) chopped fresh basil or 1 tablespoon (2 g) dried basil

2 tablespoons (30 ml) extra-virgin olive oil

⅛ teaspoon salt

1½ ounces (42 g) crumbled reduced-fat blue cheese

In your pressure cooker cooking pot, combine the water and pasta, making sure all the pasta is covered.

Lock the lid in place and close the seal valve. Press the Manual button to set the cook time for 4 minutes. When the cook time ends, use a quick pressure release.

When the valve drops, carefully remove the lid. Drain the pasta in a colander and run it under cold running water to stop the cooking process and cool it quickly. Drain well.

In a medium bowl, combine the chickpeas, tomatoes, artichoke hearts, peperoncini, red onion, basil, and olive oil. Add the drained pasta and salt. Toss well to combine.

Add the blue cheese. Gently toss to mix. Cover and refrigerate for 2 hours before serving.

YIELD: Makes about 8 cups (1.1 kg) salad

SERVES 4: About 2 cups (268 g) per serving

Nutrition Facts

SERVING SIZE (268 G)

AMOUNT PER SERVING

Calories: 290

		% Daily Value
Total Fat	10g	13%
Saturated Fat	2.5g	13%
Trans Fat	0g	
Cholesterol	5mg	2%
Sodium	700mg	30%
Total Carbohydrate	35g	13%
Dietary Fiber	3g	11%
Total Sugars	4g	
Added Sugars	0g	
Protein	12g	
Vitamin D	0mcg	
Calcium	110mg	8%
Iron	3mg	15%
Potassium	266mg	6%

LEMON-MINT CHICKEN COUSCOUS SALAD

Pearl couscous differs from the traditional tiny couscous you are likely familiar with. It's particles are the size of a pearl . . . hence its name! It tastes more like pasta than its cousin, it has more versatility because of its texture . . . and it's fun to eat, too!

2 cups (480 ml) water, plus more as needed

¾ cup (129 g) whole-wheat pearl couscous

1 pound (454 g) chicken tenders

2 teaspoons dried oregano divided

Zest of 1 lemon

Juice of 1 lemon

1 tablespoon (15 ml) extra-virgin olive oil

1 garlic clove, minced

1 tablespoon (15 ml) apple cider vinegar

¼ teaspoon salt

3 tablespoons (27 g) capers

3 ounces (85 g) crumbled reduced-fat feta cheese

½ cup (32 g) chopped fresh mint

½ cup (30 g) chopped fresh parsley

1 cup (135 g) chopped cucumber

1 lemon, quartered

In your pressure cooker cooking pot, combine the water and couscous, making sure the water covers the couscous. Top with the chicken tenders. Sprinkle with 1 teaspoon of oregano.

Lock the lid in place and close the seal valve. Press the Manual button to set the cook time for 4 minutes. When the cook time ends, use a quick pressure release.

When the valve drops, carefully remove the lid. Transfer the chicken to a cutting board and let rest for 3 to 5 minutes. Using a fine-mesh sieve, drain the couscous and run it under cold water to stop the cooking and cool it quickly. Place the couscous in a large bowl. Add the lemon zest and juice along with the olive oil, garlic, vinegar, and salt. Stir to combine.

Chop the chicken and add it to the couscous mixture. Stir in the capers, feta, mint, parsley, and cucumber. Cover and refrigerate for at least 1 hour before serving with the lemon wedges alongside for squeezing.

YIELD: Makes 5 cups (1.3 kg) salad

SERVES 4: 1¼ cups (330 g) per serving

Nutrition Facts

SERVING SIZE (196 G)

AMOUNT PER SERVING

Calories: 310

		% Daily Value
Total Fat	7g	9%
Saturated Fat	2g	10%
Trans Fat	0g	
Cholesterol	50mg	17%
Sodium	610mg	27%
Total Carbohydrate	32g	12%
Dietary Fiber	1g	4%
Total Sugars	1g	
Added Sugars	0g	
Protein	30g	
Vitamin D	0mcg	
Calcium	92mg	8%
Iron	3mg	15%
Potassium	104mg	2%

FARRO SALAD WITH SALAMI, KALE, AND OLIVE

Salami does not usually go hand in hand with the term "healthy," but, if you use it in moderation and freeze any unused portion, it can be a great flavor enhancer to have on hand and act as a seasoning agent in the dish.

2 cups (480 ml) water

1 cup (188 g) uncooked farro

2 tablespoons (30 ml) extra-virgin olive oil, divided

1 cup (150 g) chopped red bell pepper

2 ounces (55 g) hard salami slices (such as Oscar Meyer), cut into very thin strips

2 cups (134 g) finely chopped kale

2 ounces (½ cup, or 55 g) stuffed green olives, halved

3 tablespoons (45 ml) red wine vinegar

1½ teaspoons dried oregano

½ teaspoon salt

⅛ teaspoon red pepper flakes

¼ cup (25 g) grated Parmesan cheese

In your pressure cooker cooking pot, combine the water, farro, and 2 teaspoons olive oil.

Lock the lid in place and close the seal valve. Press the Manual button to set the cook time for 8 minutes. When the cook time ends, use a quick pressure release.

When the valve drops, carefully remove the lid. Drain the farro in a fine-mesh sieve and run it under cold running water to stop the cooking process and cool it quickly. Drain well and transfer to a large bowl.

Stir in the remaining ingredients, except the Parmesan cheese, until well blended. Sprinkle evenly with the cheese.

YIELD: Makes about 9 cups (1.1 kg) salad

SERVES 6: 1½ cups (127 g) per serving

Nutrition Facts

SERVING SIZE (127 G)

AMOUNT PER SERVING

Calories: **350**

		% Daily Value
Total Fat	17g	22%
Saturated Fat	4.5g	23%
Trans Fat	0g	
Cholesterol	20mg	7%
Sodium	620mg	27%
Total Carbohydrate	38g	14%
Dietary Fiber	1g	4%
Total Sugars	2g	
Added Sugars	0g	
Protein	14g	
Vitamin D	0mcg	
Calcium	128mg	10%
Iron	3mg	15%
Potassium	155mg	4%

HAM AND POTATO SALAD WITH DILL

Need a make-ahead lunch, whether for brown bagging or entertaining overnight guests?
This holds well, up to 48 hours!

Nonstick cooking spray, for preparing the cooking pot

6 ounces (170 g) lower-sodium deli ham (such as Boar's Head), chopped

2 cups (480 ml) water

1½ pounds (681 g) red potatoes, cut into ¾-inch (2 cm) cubes

½ cup (115 g) light mayonnaise

¼ cup (60 g) plain 2% Greek yogurt

½ cup (80 g) finely chopped red onion

1½ tablespoons (23 ml) apple cider vinegar

2 teaspoons dried dill

⅛ teaspoon salt

On your pressure cooker, select Sauté/Browning + more to preheat the cooking pot. Once hot, coat the pot with cooking spray. Add the ham. Cook for 4 minutes, or until it begins to brown lightly, stirring occasionally. Transfer the ham to a large bowl.

Put a steamer basket into the cooking pot and pour in the water. Place the potatoes in the basket.

Lock the lid in place and close the seal valve. Press the Cancel button. Press the Manual button to set the cook time for 4 minutes. When the cook time ends, use a quick pressure release.

When the valve drops, carefully remove the lid. Transfer the potatoes into a colander and run them under cold water to stop the cooking process and cool them quickly.

Meanwhile, add the remaining ingredients to the ham and stir until well blended. Add the potatoes and toss gently until well coated. Cover and refrigerate overnight, or for at least 8 hours.

YIELD: Makes 6 cups (1.7 kg) salad

SERVES 4: 1½ cups (278 g) per serving

Nutrition Facts

SERVING SIZE (278 G)

AMOUNT PER SERVING		
Calories:	**280**	
	% Daily Value	
Total Fat	11g	14%
Saturated Fat	0g	
Trans Fat	0g	
Cholesterol	30mg	10%
Sodium	720mg	31%
Total Carbohydrate	35g	13%
Dietary Fiber	3g	11%
Total Sugars	5g	
Added Sugars	0g	
Protein	12g	
Vitamin D	0mcg	
Calcium	37mg	2%
Iron	2mg	10%
Potassium	881mg	20%

ONE-DISH SUPPERS

All-in-one recipes have always been a priority
for people on the run, but quite often they are packed with
calories, carbs, fat, and sodium. The recipes in this section
are packed with flavor, protein, and tons of
veggies . . . they're family friendly and easy to prep, too!

ONE-DISH SUPPERS

LEMON PANKO ARTICHOKE PASTA

Tossed with freshly grated lemon zest and garlic and topped with golden crunchy bread crumbs, this creamy spinach and artichoke pasta is sure to please.

2 teaspoons extra-virgin olive oil

½ cup (25 g) panko bread crumbs

1 to 2 teaspoons grated lemon zest

¼ cup (25 g) grated Parmesan cheese, divided

½ teaspoon salt, divided

Nonstick cooking spray, for preparing the cooking pot

¾ cup (120 g) chopped onion

1 (14-ounce, or 397 g) can quartered artichoke hearts, drained

6 ounces (170 g) multigrain rotini pasta (such as Barilla Plus)

2½ cups (600 ml) water, plus more as needed

¾ teaspoon dried Italian seasoning

1 (6-ounce or 170 g) package fresh baby spinach

4 ounces (115 g) reduced-fat cream cheese, cut into small pieces

Black pepper

On your pressure cooker, select Sauté/Browning + more to preheat the cooking pot. Once hot, add the olive oil and tilt the pot to coat the bottom lightly. Add the bread crumbs. Cook for 2 minutes, or until golden, stirring constantly. Transfer the bread crumbs to a small bowl. Add the lemon zest, 1 tablespoon (6.25 g) of Parmesan cheese, and ⅛ teaspoon of salt. Toss to combine. Set aside.

Coat the cooking pot with cooking spray. Add the onion. Cook for 2 minutes.

Stir in the artichokes, pasta, water, and Italian seasoning. Mix well, making sure the pasta is covered with water.

Lock the lid in place and close the seal valve. Press the Cancel button. Press the Manual button to set the cook time for 4 minutes. When the cook time ends, use a quick pressure release.

When the valve drops, carefully remove the lid.

Nutrition Facts		
SERVING SIZE (234 G)		
AMOUNT PER SERVING		
Calories:	**350**	
	% Daily Value	
Total Fat	11g	14%
Saturated Fat	5g	25%
Trans Fat	0g	
Cholesterol	25mg	8%
Sodium	760mg	33%
Total Carbohydrate	46g	17%
Dietary Fiber	2g	7%
Total Sugars	5g	
Added Sugars	0g	
Protein	17g	
Vitamin D	0mcg	
Calcium	217mg	15%
Iron	4mg	20%
Potassium	51mg	2%

Press the Cancel button. Select Sauté/Browning + more. Add the spinach to the pasta mixture and stir until the spinach wilts, about 2 minutes.

Add the cream cheese and remaining ⅛ teaspoon of salt. Season with pepper. Bring the mixture to a boil. Cook for 4 to 5 minutes, or until thickened slightly, stirring frequently. Stir in the remaining 3 tablespoons (18.75 g) of Parmesan cheese. Serve topped with the bread crumbs.

YIELD: Makes 6 cups (1.4 kg) total

SERVES 4: 1½ cups (234 g) per serving

RUSTIC BUTTERNUT SQUASH PENNE

A rich, creamy, and gorgeous sauce made by puréeing butternut squash with half-and-half and Parmesan cheese that's tossed with penne and topped with browned shallots . . . all done in a single pot!

1 tablespoon (15 ml) canola oil

1 cup (160 g) finely chopped shallot

2 cups (480 ml) water

4 ounces (115 g) multigrain penne pasta (such as Barilla Plus)

1 (12-ounce, or 340 g) package fresh or frozen chopped butternut squash

⅔ cup (160 ml) half-and-half

½ teaspoon salt

¼ teaspoon black pepper, plus more as needed

¼ cup (25 g) grated Parmesan cheese

¼ teaspoon ground nutmeg, or to taste

On your pressure cooker, select Sauté/Browning + more to preheat the cooking pot. Once hot, add the canola oil and tilt the pot to coat the bottom lightly. Add the shallot. Cook for 3 minutes, or until just beginning to lightly brown, stirring frequently. Transfer to a plate and set aside.

Add the water and pasta to the pot. Place a steamer basket on top of the pasta and place the squash in the steamer basket.

Lock the lid in place and close the seal valve. Press the Cancel button. Press the Manual button to set the cook time for 3 minutes. When the cook time ends, use a quick pressure release.

When the valve drops, carefully remove the lid. Turn off the pressure cooker.

Remove the squash and the steamer basket from the pot. Place the squash in blender with the half-and-half. Purée until smooth.

Drain the pasta, reserving ⅔ cup (160 ml) of the cooking liquid. Return the squash purée to the pot. Stir in the pasta, reserved cooking liquid, half the shallots, the salt, pepper, and Parmesan cheese. Sprinkle lightly with nutmeg and top with the remaining shallots. Taste and season with additional pepper, if needed.

YIELD: Makes 3 cups (808 g) total

SERVES 4: ¾ cup (202 g) per serving

Nutrition Facts		
SERVING SIZE (202 G)		
AMOUNT PER SERVING		
Calories:	**250**	
	% Daily Value	
Total Fat	8g	10%
Saturated Fat	4g	20%
Trans Fat	0g	
Cholesterol	20mg	7%
Sodium	450mg	20%
Total Carbohydrate	38g	14%
Dietary Fiber	3g	11%
Total Sugars	8g	
Added Sugars	0g	
Protein	11g	
Vitamin D	0mcg	
Calcium	199mg	15%
Iron	2mg	10%
Potassium	486mg	10%

BARLEY, BROCCOLI, AND PECANS WITH BLUE CHEESE

Normally, pearl barley takes about 40 minutes to cook on the stovetop; here, it only takes 9 minutes. It's nutritious, it's packed with fiber, and it offers a unique break from pasta and rice.

2 ounces (55 g) chopped pecans or walnuts

Nonstick cooking spray, for preparing the cooking pot

6 ounces (170 g) sliced portobello mushrooms

4 ounces (115 g) pearl barley, rinsed and drained

3 cups (720 ml) water

2 bay leaves

2 cups (142 g) small (about 1-inch, or 2.5 cm) pieces broccoli florets

2 ounces (55 g) reduced-fat crumbled blue cheese or feta cheese

1 garlic clove, minced

½ teaspoon salt

On your pressure cooker, select Sauté/Browning + more to preheat the cooking pot. Once hot, add the nuts to the pot. Cook for 3 minutes, or until beginning to lightly brown, stirring occasionally. Transfer to a plate and set aside.

Coat the pressure cooker pot and the mushrooms with cooking spray. Add the mushrooms to the pot. Cook for 2 minutes per side, or until beginning to release their juices. Transfer to the plate with the nuts and set aside. Add the barley, water, and bay leaves to the pot.

Lock the lid in place and close the seal valve. Press the Cancel button. Press the Manual button to set the cook time for 9 minutes. When the cook time ends, use a quick pressure release.

When the valve drops, carefully remove the lid. Press the Cancel button. Select Sauté/Browning + more. Add the broccoli to the barley mixture. Bring to a boil. Cover the pot (do not lock the lid) and cook for 1 minute, or until the broccoli is just crisp-tender.

Drain the mixture in a fine-mesh sieve (not a colander). Return it to the pot. Stir in the mushrooms and nuts, blue cheese, garlic, and salt. Cook for 30 seconds, or until heated through.

YIELD: Makes 5 cups (556 g) total

SERVES 4: 1¼ cups (139 g) per serving

Nutrition Facts

SERVING SIZE (139 G)

AMOUNT PER SERVING

Calories: **280**

		% Daily Value
Total Fat	16g	21%
Saturated Fat	3g	15%
Trans Fat	0g	
Cholesterol	10mg	3%
Sodium	500mg	22%
Total Carbohydrate	28g	10%
Dietary Fiber	7g	25%
Total Sugars	2g	
Added Sugars	0g	
Protein	10g	
Vitamin D	0mcg	
Calcium	114mg	8%
Iron	2mg	10%
Potassium	411mg	8%

CHUNKY RATATOUILLE-STYLE VEGETABLES

These vegetables make a great topper for a multitude of foods, such as multigrain pasta, quinoa, quick-baked potatoes, grilled or skillet chicken breasts, pork chops, fish, or even portobello mushroom caps. This dish is even better the next day!

Nonstick cooking spray, for preparing the cooking pot

½ cup (80 g) finely chopped onion

1 large green bell pepper, cut into 1-inch (2.5 cm) pieces

8 ounces (225 g) whole mushrooms, quartered

8 ounces (225 g) eggplant, chopped

1 (14.5-ounce, or 410 g) can stewed tomatoes

¾ cup (180 ml) white wine

2 teaspoons dried Italian seasoning

⅛ teaspoon red pepper flakes

15 pitted Kalamata olives, coarsely chopped

1 tablespoon (16 g) tomato paste

⅛ teaspoon salt

2 (12-ounce, or 340 g) packages frozen zucchini spirals

3 ounces (85 g) shredded reduced-fat Italian cheese blend

On your pressure cooker, select Sauté/Browning + more to preheat the cooking pot. Once hot, coat the pot with cooking spray. Add the onion. Cook for 4 minutes, or until beginning to lightly brown on the edges, stirring occasionally. Stir in the green bell pepper, mushrooms, eggplant, tomatoes, wine, Italian seasoning, and red pepper flakes.

Lock the lid in place and close the seal valve. Press the Cancel button. Press the Manual button to set the cook time for 2 minutes. When the cook time ends, use a quick pressure release.

When the valve drops, carefully remove the lid. Using a slotted spoon, transfer the vegetables to a pasta bowl or large shallow bowl and set aside.

Nutrition Facts		
SERVING SIZE (487 G)		
AMOUNT PER SERVING		
Calories:	**200**	
	% Daily Value	
Total Fat	8g	10%
Saturated Fat	2.5g	13%
Trans Fat	0g	
Cholesterol	10mg	3%
Sodium	750mg	33%
Total Carbohydrate	22g	8%
Dietary Fiber	5g	18%
Total Sugars	11g	
Added Sugars	0g	
Protein	12g	
Vitamin D	0mcg	
Calcium	220mg	15%
Iron	2mg	10%
Potassium	969mg	20%

Press the Cancel button. Select Sauté/Browning + more. Bring the liquid in the pot to a boil. Stir in the olives, tomato paste, and salt. Boil for 3 to 4 minutes, or until reduced to 1 cup (240 ml). Pour the liquid over the vegetable mixture.

While the liquid reduces, prepare the zucchini spirals according to the package directions. Serve the zucchini topped with the vegetable mixture and sprinkled with the cheese.

YIELD: Makes about 3 cups (680 g) zucchini, 5 cups (944 g) vegetable mixture, 1 cup (240 ml) sauce, and ¾ cup (85 g cheese total

SERVES 4: About ¾ cup (170 g) zucchini, 1¼ cups (236 g) vegetable mixture, ¼ cup (60 ml) sauce, and 3 tablespoons (21.25 g) cheese per serving.

CHEDDAR POTATO, EDAMAME, AND FENNEL CASSEROLE

This no-bake cheesy potato main-dish casserole is topped with toasted bread crumbs. Not only does letting it stand a few minutes before serving allow the flavors to absorb but also the casserole reaches its peak "spoonable" texture.

⅓ cup (17 g) panko bread crumbs

1 cup (240 ml) water

1¼ pounds (567.5 g) red potatoes, cut into ¼-inch (0.6 cm)-thick slices

1 cup (85 g) thinly sliced fennel bulb

1 cup (150 g) fresh or frozen shelled edamame

¼ cup (60 ml) 2% milk

1½ teaspoons cornstarch

1 teaspoon garlic powder

1 teaspoon dried oregano

½ teaspoon dried thyme

¾ teaspoon salt

¼ teaspoon black pepper

5 ounces (140 g) shredded reduced-fat sharp Cheddar cheese

On your pressure cooker, select Sauté/Browning + more to preheat the cooking pot. Once hot, add the bread crumbs to the pot. Cook for 3 minutes, or until beginning to lightly brown, stirring occasionally. Transfer to a plate and set aside.

Put a steamer basket into the pot and pour in the water. Place the potatoes, fennel, and edamame in the basket.

Lock the lid in place and close the seal valve. Press the Cancel button. Press the Manual button to set the cook time for 2 minutes. When the cook time ends, use a quick pressure release.

When the valve drops, carefully remove the lid. Press the Cancel button. Select Sauté/Browning + more. Remove the vegetable mixture and the steamer basket. Place the vegetables in a shallow casserole dish.

In a small bowl, whisk the milk and cornstarch. Add this slurry to the liquid in the pot and bring to a boil. Boil for 1 minute, or until slightly thickened.

Stir in the garlic powder, oregano, thyme, salt, and pepper. Gradually add the cheese, stirring until melted and smooth. Pour the cheese sauce over the potato mixture in the casserole dish and gently toss to distribute the sauce evenly. Top with the bread crumbs. Let stand for 15 minutes to let the cheese to melt and the flavors absorb.

YIELD: Makes 6 cups (1 kg) total

SERVES 4: 1½ cups (265 g) per serving

Nutrition Facts

SERVING SIZE (265 G)

AMOUNT PER SERVING

Calories: **290**

		% Daily Value
Total Fat	9g	12%
Saturated Fat	5g	25%
Trans Fat	0g	
Cholesterol	30mg	10%
Sodium	730mg	32%
Total Carbohydrate	36g	13%
Dietary Fiber	5g	18%
Total Sugars	4g	
Added Sugars	0g	
Protein	18g	
Vitamin D	0mcg	
Calcium	358mg	30%
Iron	2mg	10%
Potassium	806mg	15%

ASIAN TWO-GRAIN BOWL

Looking for ways to add more fiber and protein to your diet? Try quinoa.
If you're unfamiliar with this grain, a nice way to introduce yourself to it is combined with
another grain, such as rice . . . then you'll be hooked!

FOR SAUCE:

¼ cup (60 ml) light soy sauce

2 tablespoons (30 ml) fresh lime juice

2 tablespoons (25 g) sugar

1 teaspoon grated peeled fresh ginger

⅛ teaspoon red pepper flakes

FOR BASE:

2 ounces (55 g) slivered almonds

½ cup (93 g) basmati rice

½ cup (92 g) quinoa

1½ cups (360 ml) water

1 cup (150 g) fresh or frozen shelled edamame, thawed if frozen

4 medium scallions, chopped

1 cup (150 g) chopped yellow bell pepper

TO MAKE THE SAUCE: In a small bowl, whisk together the sauce ingredients until combined. Set aside.

TO MAKE THE BASE: On your pressure cooker, select Sauté/Browning + more to preheat the cooking pot. Once hot, add the almonds to the pot. Cook for 4 minutes, or until beginning to lightly brown, stirring occasionally. Transfer to a plate and set aside.

Place the rice and quinoa into the pot. Carefully add the water.

Lock the lid in place and close the seal valve. Press the Cancel button. Press the Manual button to set the cook time for 4 minutes. When the cook time ends, use a quick pressure release.

When the valve drops, carefully remove the lid. Stir in the edamame, scallions, and yellow bell pepper. Cover the pot and let stand for 2 minutes.

Stir the sauce and spoon it over the rice mixture. Sprinkle with the toasted almonds.

YIELD: Makes 5 cups (843 g) rice mixture, ½ cup nuts (55 g), and ½ cup (120 ml) sauce

SERVES 4: 1¼ cups rice mixture (255 g), 2 tablespoons (13.75 g) nuts, and 2 tablespoons (30 ml) sauce per serving

Nutrition Facts

SERVING SIZE (166 G)

AMOUNT PER SERVING

Calories: **330**

		% Daily Value
Total Fat	10g	13%
Saturated Fat	0.5g	3%
Trans Fat	0g	
Cholesterol	0mg	
Sodium	590mg	26%
Total Carbohydrat	46g	17%
Dietary Fiber	5g	18%
Total Sugars	5g	
Added Sugars	2g	4%
Protein	13g	
Vitamin D	0mcg	
Calcium	76mg	6%
Iron	3mg	15%
Potassium	310mg	6%

MIDDLE EASTERN SPICED TOMATO COUSCOUS

Pearl couscous, also known as Israeli couscous, has a more distinct, chewy pasta texture than its tiny cousin. It also takes longer to cook. Try replacing the pasta in your pasta salad recipes with pearl couscous—just chop the other ingredients a little smaller to balance the dish.

1 teaspoon canola oil

½ cup (80 g) finely chopped onion

½ cup slivered almonds (55 g) or pine nuts (68 g)

1 (14.5-ounce, or 410 g) can stewed tomatoes

½ cup (86 g) pearl couscous

¾ cup (180 ml) water

½ cup (114 g) pimiento-stuffed olives

⅓ cup (50 g) raisins

1 teaspoon ground cumin

⅛ teaspoon cayenne pepper

½ (15-ounce, or 425 g) can no-salt-added chickpeas, rinsed and drained

⅓ cup (5 g) chopped fresh cilantro

2 teaspoons grated peeled fresh ginger

¼ teaspoon salt

On your pressure cooker, select Sauté/Browning + more to preheat the cooking pot. Once hot, add the canola oil and tilt the pot to coat the bottom lightly. Add the onion and almonds. Cook for 5 minutes until lightly browned, stirring frequently. Stir in the tomatoes, couscous, water, olives, raisins, cumin, and cayenne.

Lock the lid in place and close the seal valve. Press the Cancel button. Press the Manual button to set the cook time for 4 minutes. When the cook time ends, use a quick pressure release.

When the valve drops, carefully remove the lid. Stir in the chickpeas, cilantro, ginger, and salt, breaking up any larger pieces of tomato that remain with a fork. Cover, do not lock the lid, and let stand for 5 minutes to absorb the flavors and allow the couscous to continue cooking.

YIELD: Makes 4 cups (1.1 kg) couscous

SERVES 4: 1 cup (275 g) per serving

Cook's Note
For a thinner consistency, after letting stand for 5 minutes, add ¼ to ⅓ cup (60 to 80 ml) of water.

Nutrition Facts
SERVING SIZE (220 G)

AMOUNT PER SERVING
Calories: **290**

		% Daily Value
Total Fat	11g	14%
Saturated Fat	0.5g	3%
Trans Fat	0g	
Cholesterol	0mg	
Sodium	630mg	27%
Total Carbohydrate	40g	15%
Dietary Fiber	3g	11%
Total Sugars	12g	
Added Sugars	0g	
Protein	8g	
Vitamin D	0mcg	
Calcium	81mg	6%
Iron	2mg	10%
Potassium	283mg	6%

WARM QUINOA AND KALE BLACK BEAN BOWLS

Deep, dark black beans are cooked with quinoa, served with a warm jalapeño-citrus oil, and topped with chunks of avocado. A striking presentation.

4 ounces (115 g) dried black beans, rinsed

4 cups (960 ml) water

½ cup (92 g) quinoa

2 cups (85 g) baby kale mix

1 jalapeño pepper, seeded and minced

2 tablespoons (30 ml) extra-virgin olive oil

2 tablespoons (30 ml) fresh lemon juice

1 garlic clove, minced

¾ teaspoon salt

1 avocado, peeled, pitted, and chopped

In your pressure cooker cooking pot, combine the black beans and water.

Lock the lid in place and close the seal valve. Press the Manual button to set the cook time for 18 minutes. When the cook time ends, use a quick pressure release.

When the valve drops, carefully remove the lid. Stir in the quinoa.

Lock the lid in place and close the seal valve. Press the Cancel button. Press the Manual button to set the cook time for 1 minute. When the cook time ends, use a quick pressure release.

When the valve drops, carefully remove the lid. Drain the bean mixture in a fine-mesh sieve (not a colander), discarding the liquid. Place the bean mixture in a shallow bowl. Add the kale mix. Toss until well blended.

In a small bowl, whisk the jalapeño, olive oil, lemon juice, garlic, and salt.

Press the Cancel button. Select Sauté/Browning + more. Pour the jalapeño mixture into the cooking pot and bring it to a boil. Cook for 1 minute, or until it reduces to ¼ cup (60 ml). Spoon the liquid evenly over the bean mixture. *Do not stir*. Top with the avocado.

YIELD: Makes 4 cups (300 g) bean mixture, ¼ cup (60 ml) sauce, and about 1 cup (146 g) avocado

SERVES 4: 1 cup (75 g) bean mixture, 1 tablespoon (15 ml) sauce, and about ¼ cup (36.5 g) avocado per serving

Nutrition Facts

SERVING SIZE (126 G)

AMOUNT PER SERVING

Calories: **340**

		% Daily Value
Total Fat	17g	22%
Saturated Fat	2.5g	13%
Trans Fat	0g	
Cholesterol	0mg	
Sodium	450mg	20%
Total Carbohydrate	38g	14%
Dietary Fiber	5g	18%
Total Sugars	5g	
Added Sugars	0g	
Protein	10g	
Vitamin D	0mcg	
Calcium	98mg	8%
Iron	4mg	20%
Potassium	796mg	15%

Cook's Note

This can be served in 4 individual shallow bowls, if desired, either hot or cold.

TWO-CHEESE CAULIFLOWER ROTINI

When you see a recipe that calls for sharp Cheddar cheese, you usually think of the yellow-orange variety. But the white variety is widely available and gives a new dimension of flavor and color . . . for the same number of calories and fat grams. It's an interesting addition for the same nutritional "price."

4 ounces (115 g) multigrain rotini (such as Barilla Plus)

1½ cups (360 ml) water, plus more as needed

2 cups (200 g) small (about 1-inch, or 2.5 cm) cauliflower florets

¼ cup (60 ml) 2% milk

1 teaspoon cornstarch

½ teaspoon Dijon mustard

1 small red bell pepper, cut in into thin strips, about 2 inches (5 cm) long

½ teaspoon salt

Pinch cayenne pepper

3 ounces (85 g) reduced-fat sharp white or yellow Cheddar cheese, shredded

1 ounce (28 g) sliced Swiss cheese, torn into small pieces

Black pepper

In your pressure cooker cooking pot, combine the rotini and water, making sure all the pasta is covered with water.

Lock the lid in place and close the seal valve. Press the Manual button to set the cook time for 3 minutes. When the cook time ends, use a quick pressure release.

When the valve drops, carefully remove the lid. Stir in the cauliflower.

In a small bowl, whisk the milk, cornstarch, and mustard until the cornstarch dissolves. Stir this slurry into the cauliflower mixture.

Press the Cancel button. Select Sauté/Browning + more. Bring the mixture to a boil. Cook, uncovered, for 4 minutes, or until the cauliflower is just crisp-tender, stirring occasionally. Turn off the pressure cooker.

Stir in the red bell pepper, salt, and cayenne until well blended. Gradually add the cheeses, stirring to combine. Sprinkle with the black pepper.

YIELD: Makes 4 cups (840 g) total

SERVES 4: 1 cup (210 g) per serving

Cook's Note

For a thinner consistency, add 1 to 2 tablespoons (15 to 30 ml) more milk at the end.

Nutrition Facts

SERVING SIZE (120 G)

AMOUNT PER SERVING

Calories: **220**

		% Daily Value
Total Fat	8g	10%
Saturated Fat	4.5g	23%
Trans Fat	0g	
Cholesterol	20mg	7%
Sodium	570mg	25%
Total Carbohydrate	24g	9%
Dietary Fiber	1g	4%
Total Sugars	3g	
Added Sugars	0g	
Protein	13g	
Vitamin D	0mcg	
Calcium	252mg	20%
Iron	2mg	10%
Potassium	167mg	4%

BROCCOLI WALNUT RICE BOWLS

To toss or not to toss—that's the dilemma we often encounter when served those popular "bowls." *don't* toss this one after it has been assembled. You want the layers of flavors to be distinct!

Nonstick cooking spray, for preparing the cooking pot

1 cup (160 g) chopped onion

1⅓ cups (320 ml) water

1 cup (190 g) brown rice

2 garlic cloves, sliced lengthwise

2 cups (142 g) small (about 1-inch, or 2.5 cm) broccoli florets

3 ounces (85 g) chopped walnuts

¼ teaspoon salt

2 tablespoons (30 ml) light soy sauce

1 teaspoon sesame oil

1½ teaspoons Sriracha

On your pressure cooker, select Sauté/Browning + more to preheat the cooking pot. Once hot, coat the pot with cooking spray. Add the onion and coat it with cooking spray. Cook for 10 minutes, or until beginning to richly brown, stirring occasionally. Transfer to a plate and set aside.

Add the water, rice, and garlic to the pot.

Lock the lid in place and close the seal valve. Press the Cancel button. Press the Manual button to set the cook time for 22 minutes. When the cook time ends, use a natural pressure release for 10 minutes, then a quick pressure release.

When the valve drops, carefully remove the lid. Stir in the broccoli. Cover the pot, do not lock the lid, and let stand for 4 minutes.

Stir in the cooked onion, walnuts, and salt. Divide the rice among 4 individual bowls. Spoon the soy sauce evenly over each. Drizzle evenly with the sesame oil and Sriracha.

YIELD: Makes 5⅓ cups (940 g) total

SERVES 4: 1⅓ cups (226 g) per serving

Nutrition Facts

SERVING SIZE (146 G)

AMOUNT PER SERVING

Calories: **350**

		% Daily Value
Total Fat	17g	22%
Saturated Fat	2g	10%
Trans Fat	0g	
Cholesterol	0mg	
Sodium	500mg	22%
Total Carbohydrate	44g	16%
Dietary Fiber	4g	14%
Total Sugars	3g	
Added Sugars	0g	
Protein	9g	
Vitamin D	0mcg	
Calcium	48mg	4%
Iron	2mg	10%
Potassium	362mg	8%

SHRIMP AND SMOKED SAUSAGE CAJUN RICE

No need to finely chop onions, peppers, and tomatoes . . . the picante sauce does it for you!

Nonstick cooking spray, for preparing the cooking pot

4 ounces (115 g) smoked turkey sausage, thinly sliced

2½ cups (600 ml) water, divided

¾ cup (143 g) brown rice

1 teaspoon chipotle powder

½ teaspoon dried thyme

1 bay leaf

⅔ cup (160 ml) picante sauce

12 ounces (340 g) peeled and deveined shrimp, fresh or frozen

⅔ cup (87 g) frozen green peas

1 tablespoon (15 ml) extra-virgin olive oil

On your pressure cooker, select Sauté/Browning + more to preheat the cooking pot. Once hot, coat the pressure cooker pot with cooking spray. Add the sausage. Cook for 5 minutes, or until beginning to lightly brown, stirring occasionally. Transfer to a plate and set aside.

In the cooking pot, combine 2 cups (480 ml) of water and the rice, chipotle powder, thyme, and bay leaf.

Lock the lid in place and close the seal valve. Press the Cancel button. Press the Manual button to set the cook time for 20 minutes. When the cook time ends, use a quick pressure release.

When the valve drops, carefully remove the lid. Press the Cancel button. Select Sauté/Browning + more. Stir in the picante sauce, shrimp, cooked sausage, frozen peas, and remaining ½ cup (120 ml) of water. Make sure the shrimp are submerged. Bring the mixture to a boil. Cook for 5 minutes, or until the shrimp are opaque in the center, stirring frequently. Turn off the pressure cooker and stir in the olive oil. Let stand, uncovered, for 10 minutes.

YIELD: Makes 6 cups (1.35 kg) total

SERVES 4: 1½ cups (337 g) per serving

Cook's Note

Letting the mixture stand for a few minutes releases any browned bits on the bottom of the pot, and their flavor, that formed during the cooking process.

Nutrition Facts		
SERVING SIZE (337 G)		
AMOUNT PER SERVING		
Calories:	**320**	
	% Daily Value	
Total Fat	7g	9%
Saturated Fat	1g	5%
Trans Fat	0g	
Cholesterol	115mg	38%
Sodium	690mg	30%
Total Carbohydrate	46g	17%
Dietary Fiber	3g	11%
Total Sugars	2g	
Added Sugars	0g	
Protein	18g	
Vitamin D	0mcg	
Calcium	53mg	4%
Iron	2mg	10%
Potassium	202mg	4%

SHRIMP-OKRA CREOLE WITH RICE

With only 220 calories and 1 gram of fat, there's no room for concern here! Simply enjoy every bite!

2 cups (300 g) chopped green bell pepper

1 cup (160 g) chopped onion

1 cup (100 g) sliced celery

2 cups (600 g) fresh or frozen cut okra

1 (14.5-ounce, or 410 g) can diced fire-roasted tomatoes with garlic

¾ cup (180 ml) water

2 bay leaves

1 teaspoon dried thyme

½ teaspoon garlic powder

¼ cup (65 g) tomato paste

1 pound (454 g) fresh or frozen peeled and deveined shrimp

1 tablespoon (15 ml) hot sauce (such as Frank's)

1 teaspoon salt

¼ teaspoon black pepper

1 tablespoon (15 ml) extra-virgin olive oil

3 cups (340 g) cooked rice

In your pressure cooker cooking pot, combine the green bell pepper, onion, celery, okra, tomatoes, water, bay leaves, thyme, and garlic powder. Spoon the tomato paste on top of the mixture. *Do not stir.*

Lock the lid in place and close the seal valve. Press the Manual button to set the cook time for 20 minutes. When the cook time ends, use a quick pressure release.

When the valve drops, carefully remove the lid. Press the Cancel button. Select Sauté/Browning + more. Stir in the shrimp, hot sauce, salt, and pepper. Bring to a boil. Cook for 5 minutes, or until the shrimp are opaque in the center, stirring frequently. Turn off the pressure cooker and stir in the olive oil. Let stand, uncovered, for 5 minutes. Serve over rice.

YIELD: Makes 6 cups (1.9 kg) shrimp mixture plus 3 cups (55 g) cooked rice total.

SERVES 6: 1 cup (310 g) shrimp mixture plus ½ cup (56 g) rice per serving

Cook's Note
Leftovers? Freeze them! It's best to freeze the shrimp mixture and rice in separate containers.

Nutrition Facts
SERVING SIZE (365 G)

AMOUNT PER SERVING

Calories: **220**

		% Daily Value
Total Fat	1g	1%
Saturated Fat	0g	
Trans Fat	0g	
Cholesterol	95mg	32%
Sodium	830mg	36%
Total Carbohydrate	36g	13%
Dietary Fiber	4g	14%
Total Sugars	6g	
Added Sugars	0g	
Protein	15g	
Vitamin D	0mcg	
Calcium	121mg	10%
Iron	3mg	15%
Potassium	537mg	10%

CHEESY CHICKEN AND POBLANO RICE

Turmeric added during cooking gives the rice a bright yellow color, which gives the dish a "cheesier" appearance without overdoing the fat and calories.

1 teaspoon canola oil

2 cups (236 g) chopped poblano chile (from about 4 chiles)

12 ounces (340 g) boneless, skinless chicken breast, cut into bite-size pieces

¾ cup (139 g) long-grain white rice

¾ cup (180 ml) water

2 teaspoons ground cumin, divided

¼ teaspoon ground turmeric

3 ounces (85 g) shredded reduced-fat Mexican cheese blend

¾ teaspoon salt

¼ teaspoon black pepper

On your pressure cooker, select Sauté/Browning + more to preheat the cooking pot. Once hot, add the canola oil and tilt the pot to coat the bottom lightly. Add the poblanos. Cook for 8 minutes, stirring occasionally. (Note: Do not stir often; you want a "roasted" pepper effect.) Add the chicken in a single layer. Cook for 2 minutes, *without stirring*.

Stir in the rice, the water, 1 teaspoon of cumin, and the turmeric.

Lock the lid in place and close the seal valve. Press the Cancel button. Press the Manual button to set the cook time for 4 minutes. When the cook time ends, use a natural pressure release for 10 minutes, then a quick pressure release.

When the valve drops, carefully remove the lid. Stir in the remaining 1 teaspoon of cumin and the cheese, salt, and pepper.

YIELD: Makes 5 cups (1.2 kg) total

SERVES 4: 1¼ cups (300 g) per serving

Nutrition Facts
SERVING SIZE (300 G)

AMOUNT PER SERVING

Calories: 350

		% Daily Value
Total Fat	8g	10%
Saturated Fat	3.5g	18%
Trans Fat	0g	
Cholesterol	75mg	25%
Sodium	630mg	27%
Total Carbohydrate	39g	14%
Dietary Fiber	2g	7%
Total Sugars	4g	
Added Sugars	0g	
Protein	30g	
Vitamin D	0mcg	
Calcium	220mg	15%
Iron	3mg	15%
Potassium	611mg	15%

CHICKEN AND NEW POTATOES WITH LEMONY SAUCE

Look for "petite Yukon gold" potatoes sold in bags. They are colorful, creamy, and moist . . . and the perfect size!

---

1 lemon, cut into 8 wedges

6 garlic cloves, peeled

1 cup (240 ml) water

1 teaspoon paprika

½ teaspoon poultry seasoning or 1 teaspoon dried thyme

1 teaspoon onion powder

½ teaspoon black pepper

¾ teaspoon salt, divided

4 (about 2 pounds, or 908 g, total) bone-in skinless chicken thighs

12 ounces (340 g) petite red or Yukon gold potatoes, about 1 inch (2.5 cm) in diameter

In your pressure cooker cooking pot, combine the lemon, garlic, and water. In a small bowl, stir together the paprika, poultry seasoning, onion powder, pepper, and ¼ teaspoon of salt. Place the chicken on top of the lemons. Sprinkle with the paprika mixture.

Lock the lid in place and close the seal valve. Press the Manual button to set the cook time for 15 minutes. When the cook time ends, use a quick pressure release.

When the valve drops, carefully remove the lid. Remove the chicken and lemons from the pot and place them on a serving platter. Cover with aluminum foil to keep warm.

Add the potatoes and remaining ½ teaspoon of salt to the liquid in the pot.

Lock the lid in place and close the seal valve. Press the Cancel button. Press the Manual button to set the cook time for 3 minutes. When the cook time ends, use a quick pressure release.

When the valve drops, carefully remove the lid.

(continued)

Nutrition Facts		
SERVING SIZE (317 G)		
AMOUNT PER SERVING		
Calories:	**340**	
	% Daily Value	
Total Fat	9g	12%
Saturated Fat	2.5g	13%
Trans Fat	0g	
Cholesterol	215mg	72%
Sodium	670mg	29%
Total Carbohydrate	15g	5%
Dietary Fiber	2g	7%
Total Sugars	1g	
Added Sugars	0g	
Protein	46g	
Vitamin D	0mcg	0%
Calcium	33mg	2%
Iron	3mg	15%
Potassium	954mg	20%

Press the Cancel button. Select Sauté/Browning + more. Bring the liquid to a boil and boil for 5 minutes to thicken the sauce slightly. Spoon the potatoes and sauce over the chicken.

YIELD: Makes 4 chicken thighs, 12 ounces (680 g) potatoes, and about 1 cup (240 ml) sauce

SERVES 4: 1 chicken thigh, 3 ounces (170 g) potatoes, and about ¼ cup (60 ml) sauce per serving

Cook's Note

For a thicker sauce, combine 1 tablespoon (15 ml) cold water and 1 tablespoon (8 g) cornstarch and stir until dissolved. Add to the boiling liquid and boil for 1 minute.

SPICY PINEAPPLE CHICKEN AND SNOW PEAS

No need for rice here. The combination of chicken and pineapple surrounded by
snow peas and peppers, topped with a sweet ginger soy sauce and peanuts, is definitely
all that's needed . . . and all done in one pot!

FOR SAUCE:

3 tablespoons (45 ml) light soy sauce

2 tablespoons (25 g) sugar

1½ tablespoons (23 ml) apple cider vinegar

2 teaspoons grated peeled fresh ginger

⅛ teaspoon red pepper flakes

FOR CHICKEN:

1 ounce (28 g) unsalted peanuts

1 tablespoon (15 ml) canola oil

12 ounces (340 g) boneless, skinless chicken thighs, trimmed and cut into 1-inch (2.5 cm) cubes

1 cup (160 g) coarsely chopped onion

2 (8-ounce, or 225 g) cans pineapple chunks in their own juice

½ teaspoon curry powder

¼ teaspoon salt

4 ounces (115 g) fresh snow peas, trimmed

1 medium red bell pepper, thinly sliced

TO MAKE THE SAUCE: In a small bowl, whisk all the sauce ingredients to combine and set aside.

TO MAKE THE CHICKEN: On your pressure cooker, select Sauté/Browning + more to preheat the cooking pot. Once hot, add the peanuts to the pot. Cook for 4 minutes, or until beginning to lightly brown. Remove from the pot and set aside.

Add the canola oil and tilt the pot to coat the bottom lightly. Add the chicken. *Do not stir.* Cook for 5 minutes. Add the onion, pineapple and juice, curry powder, and salt. Stir to blend.

Lock the lid in place and close the seal valve. Press the Cancel button. Press the Manual button to set the cook time for 4 minutes. Quick release. When the valve drops, carefully remove the lid. Using a slotted spoon, transfer the ingredients to a rimmed platter or shallow pasta bowl. Cover to keep warm.

Add the snow peas and red bell pepper to the liquid in pot.

(continued)

Nutrition Facts

SERVING SIZE (351 G)

AMOUNT PER SERVING

Calories: **340**

		% Daily Value
Total Fat	13g	17%
Saturated Fat	2.5g	13%
Trans Fat	0g	
Cholesterol	55mg	18%
Sodium	630mg	27%
Total Carbohydrate	33g	12%
Dietary Fiber	4g	14%
Total Sugars	26g	
Added Sugars	6g	12%
Protein	21g	
Vitamin D	0mcg	
Calcium	37mg	2%
Iron	2mg	10%
Potassium	562mg	10%

Lock the lid in place and close the seal valve. Press the Cancel button. Press the Manual button to set the cook time for 1 minute. When the cook time ends, use a quick pressure release.

When the valve drops, carefully remove the lid. Using a slotted spoon, remove the vegetables and arrange them around the chicken mixture. Drizzle the sauce over the chicken mixture, and sprinkle with the peanuts.

YIELD: Makes 6 cups (1.2 kg) total

SERVES 4: 1½ cups (314 g) chicken mixture and vegetables, 2 tablespoons (30 ml) sauce, and 1 tablespoon (7 g) peanuts per serving

WHOLE CHICKEN WITH VEGETABLES

This is your go-to recipe whenever you need a "roast" chicken that's extra juicy and tender . . . the knife "melts" through the chicken breast while you slice it!

---

1 teaspoon paprika

½ teaspoon poultry seasoning

½ teaspoon garlic powder

½ teaspoon salt, divided

8 ounces (225 g) carrots, cut into 2-inch (5 cm) pieces

1 onion, cut into 8 wedges

2 celery stalks, cut into 2-inch (5 cm) pieces

1 cup (240 ml) water

1 lemon, quartered

1 tablespoon (15 ml) canola oil

1 (4-pound, or 1.8 kg) whole fryer chicken

¼ teaspoon black pepper

In a small bowl, stir together the paprika, poultry seasoning, garlic powder, and ¼ teaspoon of salt. Set aside.

In your pressure cooker cooking pot, combine the carrots, onion, celery, and water. Place the lemon into the chicken's cavity. Rub the canola oil evenly over the chicken and sprinkle it with the paprika mixture. Place the chicken on top of the vegetables in the pot.

Lock the lid in place and close the seal valve. Press the Manual button to set the cook time for 25 minutes. When the cook time ends, use a quick pressure release.

Nutrition Facts		
SERVING SIZE (363 G)		
AMOUNT PER SERVING		
Calories:	**340**	
	% Daily Value	
Total Fat	10g	13%
Saturated Fat	2g	10%
Trans Fat	0g	
Cholesterol	150mg	50%
Sodium	530mg	23%
Total Carbohydrate	12g	4%
Dietary Fiber	3g	11%
Total Sugars	6g	
Added Sugars	0g	
Protein	48g	
Vitamin D	0mcg	
Calcium	68mg	6%
Iron	2mg	10%
Potassium	828mg	20%

When the valve drops, carefully remove the lid. Using 2 large spoons or a spoon and fork, carefully remove the chicken and let stand for 15 minutes before slicing, discarding the skin.

Using a slotted spoon, remove the vegetables and place them around the sliced chicken. Sprinkle all with the remaining ¼ teaspoon of salt and the pepper.

YIELD: Makes one chicken and 3 cups (455 g) vegetables total

SERVES 4: ¼ chicken and ¾ cup (170 g) vegetables per serving

CREAMY CHICKEN-PIMIENTO PASTA

Serve dinner in a hurry (and be colorful about it!) with tender chunks of chicken thigh meat, pasta, mixed veggies, and pimiento swimming in *two* kinds of cheese!

8 ounces (225 g) boneless, skinless chicken thighs, cut into bite-size pieces

4 ounces (115 g) multigrain rotini

2 cups (364 g) frozen mixed vegetables

1 cup (240 ml) reduced-sodium chicken broth

1 cup (240 ml) water

½ teaspoon dried thyme

2 ounces (55 g) shredded reduced-fat sharp Cheddar cheese, divided

3 ounces (85 g) reduced-fat cream cheese, cut into small pieces

1 (7-ounce, or 200 g) jar sliced pimientos

½ teaspoon salt

¼ teaspoon black pepper

⅛ teaspoon cayenne pepper (optional)

In your pressure cooker cooking pot, combine the chicken, rotini, frozen vegetables, chicken broth, water, and thyme.

Lock the lid in place and close the seal valve. Press the Manual button to set the cook time for 4 minutes. When the cook time ends, use a natural pressure release for 5 minutes, then a quick pressure release.

When the valve drops, carefully remove the lid. Turn off the pressure cooker.

In a small bowl, stir together 1 ounce (28 g) of Cheddar cheese and the cream cheese, pimientos, salt, black pepper, and cayenne (if using). Gradually stir the cream cheese mixture into the chicken mixture until the cheese melts. Sprinkle with the remaining Cheddar cheese.

YIELD: Makes 6 cups (1.2 kg) total

SERVES 4: 1½ cups (295 g) per serving

Nutrition Facts

SERVING SIZE (295 G)

AMOUNT PER SERVING

Calories: **330**

		% Daily Value
Total Fat	10g	13%
Saturated Fat	5g	25%
Trans Fat	0g	
Cholesterol	80mg	27%
Sodium	690mg	30%
Total Carbohydrate	35g	13%
Dietary Fiber	1g	4%
Total Sugars	7g	
Added Sugars	0g	
Protein	25g	
Vitamin D	0mcg	
Calcium	172mg	15%
Iron	3mg	15%
Potassium	276mg	6%

SCALLION CHICKEN AND RICE

Super fast, super easy, super comforting. You don't even have to remove the chicken from the pot to pull it apart! See? Comfort doesn't have to be hard!

1 cup (160 g) chopped onion

2/3 cup (160 ml) water

1 pound (454 g) boneless, skinless chicken thighs, trimmed of fat

3 tablespoons (45 ml) light soy sauce, divided

1 tablespoon (8 g) cornstarch

½ cup (65 g) frozen green peas

1 (8.8-ounce, or 249.5 g) pouch cooked brown rice (such as Uncle Ben's Ready Rice)

½ cup (50 g) chopped scallion

In your pressure cooker cooking pot, combine the onion and water. Top with the chicken in a single layer. Spoon 2 tablespoons (30 ml) of soy sauce over all.

Lock the lid in place and close the seal valve. Press the Manual button to set the cook time for 10 minutes. When the cook time ends, use a quick pressure release.

When the valve drops, carefully remove the lid.

In a small bowl, stir together the remaining 1 tablespoon (15 ml) of soy sauce and the cornstarch, stirring until the cornstarch dissolves. Add this slurry to the pot. Add the frozen peas.

Press the Cancel button. Select Sauté/Browning + more. Bring the liquid to a boil. Cook for 1 to 2 minutes, or until slightly thickened. Using 2 forks, pull apart the chicken into smaller pieces (do *not* shred).

Prepare the rice according to the package directions. Serve the chicken over the rice and top with chopped scallion.

YIELD: Makes 3 cups (680 g) chicken mixture, 2 cups (200 g) rice, and ½ cup (50 g) scallion total

SERVES 4: ¾ cup (168 g) chicken mixture, ½ cup (50 g) rice, and 2 tablespoons (12.5 g) scallion per serving

Nutrition Facts		
SERVING SIZE (230 G)		
AMOUNT PER SERVING		
Calories:	**310**	
	% Daily Value	
Total Fat	10g	13%
Saturated Fat	2.5g	13%
Trans Fat	0g	
Cholesterol	75mg	25%
Sodium	510mg	22%
Total Carbohydrate	25g	9%
Dietary Fiber	2g	7%
Total Sugars	2g	
Added Sugars	0g	
Protein	24g	
Vitamin D	0mcg	
Calcium	28mg	2%
Iron	2mg	10%
Potassium	292mg	6%

PROVENÇAL GARLIC CHICKEN

Not crazy about the thought of peeling two dozen garlic cloves? You can purchase them peeled!
Look for them in the produce section of your supermarket.

1 Tablespoon (15 ml) canola oil

24 garlic cloves, peeled (about 2 heads)

4 bone-in chicken thighs, skin removed, trimmed of fat

4 chicken drumsticks, skin removed

1 cup (240 ml) dry white wine

Paprika, for seasoning

½ teaspoon dried thyme

¼ teaspoon dried rosemary (optional)

½ teaspoon salt

¼ teaspoon black pepper

On your pressure cooker, select Sauté/Browning + more to preheat the cooking pot. Once hot, add the canola oil and the garlic. Cook until golden brown, stirring constantly. Top with the chicken and wine. Season to taste with paprika and sprinkle on the thyme and rosemary (if using).

Lock the lid in place and close the seal valve. Press the Cancel button. Press the Manual button to set the cook time for 15 minutes. When the cook time ends, use a natural pressure release for 5 minutes, then a quick pressure release.

When the valve drops, carefully remove the lid. Using a slotted spoon, transfer the chicken to a platter.

Press the Cancel button. Select Sauté/Browning + more. Add the salt and pepper. Bring the liquid to a boil and cook 7 for 8 minutes until reduced to 1⅓ cups (320 ml).

Serve chicken and sauce in shallow bowls to contain the flavorful sauce.

YIELD: Makes 4 thighs, 4 drumsticks, and 1⅓ cups (320 ml) sauce total

SERVES 4: 1 thigh, 1 drumstick, and ⅓ cup (80 ml) sauce per serving

---

Nutrition Facts

SERVING SIZE (232 G)

AMOUNT PER SERVING

Calories: **340**

		% Daily Value
Total Fat	15g	19%
Saturated Fat	3.5g	18%
Trans Fat	0g	
Cholesterol	160mg	53%
Sodium	500mg	22%
Total Carbohydrate	7g	3%
Dietary Fiber	0g	
Total Sugars	0g	
Added Sugars	0g	
Protein	39g	
Vitamin D	0mcg	
Calcium	52mg	4%
Iron	2mg	10%
Potassium	468mg	10%

INDIAN-SPICED GINGER CHICKEN

When shopping for fresh ginger, don't feel like you have to buy a big piece. Simply break off a portion—a 1-inch (2.5 cm) piece will yield about 1 teaspoon grated ginger.

1 tablespoon (15 ml) canola oil

1 pound (454 g) boneless, skinless chicken thighs, trimmed of fat, quartered

1¼ cups (312.5 g) tomato purée

½ cup (120 ml) water

2 teaspoons ground cumin, divided

1½ teaspoons paprika

½ teaspoon salt

¼ teaspoon red pepper flakes

1 tablespoon (8 g) grated peeled fresh ginger

2 tablespoons (28 g) light butter with canola oil

¼ cup (4 g) chopped fresh cilantro

2 to 3 teaspoons sugar

1 teaspoon garam masala

On your pressure cooker, select Sauté/Browning + more to preheat the cooking pot. Once hot, add the canola oil and tilt the pot to coat the bottom lightly. Add half the chicken pieces and cook, without stirring, for 3 minutes on one side. Remove from the pot and set aside. Repeat with the remaining chicken. (Note: Residue may build up on the bottom of the pot, but that adds flavor to the dish.). Return the browned chicken to the pot and gently stir in the tomato purée, water, 1 teaspoon of cumin, the paprika, salt, and red pepper flakes.

Lock the lid in place and close the seal valve. Press the Cancel button. Press the Manual button to set the cook time for 5 minutes. When the cook time ends, use a natural pressure release for 10 minutes, then a quick pressure release.

When the valve drops, carefully remove the lid. Stir in the remaining 1 teaspoon of cumin along with the ginger, butter, cilantro, sugar, and garam masala. Serve in bowls to contain the flavorful sauce.

YIELD: Makes about 4 cups (1 kg) chicken mixture total

SERVES 4: 1 cup (253 g) per serving

Nutrition Facts

SERVING SIZE (253 G)

AMOUNT PER SERVING

Calories: **350**

		% Daily Value
Total Fat	13g	17%
Saturated Fat	3.5g	18%
Trans Fat	0g	
Cholesterol	80mg	27%
Sodium	550mg	24%
Total Carbohydrate	31g	11%
Dietary Fiber	2g	7%
Total Sugars	6g	
Added Sugars	2g	4%
Protein	24g	
Vitamin D	0mcg	
Calcium	31mg	2%
Iron	4mg	20%
Potassium	522mg	10%

CHICKEN AND WILD RICE PILAF

The earthy combination of wild rice, brown rice, pumpkin seeds, and poultry seasoning is tied together with a handful of dried cherries . . . a taste of autumn in every bite! This can be served at room temperature as well.

⅔ cup (107 g) wild rice

⅓ cup (63 g) brown rice

1½ cups (360 ml) fat-free, reduced-sodium chicken broth

1½ cups (360 ml) water

Nonstick cooking spray, for preparing the cooking pot

8 ounces (225 g) boneless, skinless chicken breast, chopped

1½ ounces (43 g) roasted hulled pumpkin seeds

¼ cup (40 g) dried cherries

¼ cup (25 g) chopped scallion

1 tablespoon (15 ml) extra-virgin olive oil

½ teaspoon poultry seasoning

½ teaspoon salt

In your pressure cooker cooking pot, combine the wild rice, brown rice, chicken broth, and water.

Lock the lid in place and close the seal valve. Press the Manual button to set the cook time for 20 minutes. When the cook time ends, use a quick pressure release.

When the valve drops, carefully remove the lid. In a fine-mesh sieve, drain the rice mixture and set aside.

Press the Cancel button. Select Sauté/Browning + more and coat the pot with cooking spray. Add the chicken. Cook for 3 minutes, or until the chicken is no longer pink in the center, stirring occasionally. Turn off the pressure cooker. Stir in the drained rice mixture and the remaining ingredients.

YIELD: Makes 4 cups (1.2 kg)

SERVES 4: 1 cup (242 g) per serving

Nutrition Facts

SERVING SIZE (242 G)

AMOUNT PER SERVING

Calories: **330**

		% Daily Value
Total Fat	11g	14%
Saturated Fat	2g	10%
Trans Fat	0g	
Cholesterol	40mg	13%
Sodium	510mg	22%
Total Carbohydrate	40g	15%
Dietary Fiber	4g	14%
Total Sugars	7g	
Added Sugars	0g	
Protein	21g	
Vitamin D	0mcg	
Calcium	25mg	2%
Iron	2mg	10%
Potassium	467mg	10%

SHEET-PAN CUMIN TURKEY WITH TORTILLA CHIPS

Friday nights were made for this! So is Monday-night football watching! This will definitely be your pick when it's time for fun!!!

12 ounces (340 g) 93% lean ground turkey

2 teaspoons chili powder

1 teaspoon ground cumin

½ (15-ounce, or 425 g) can no-salt-added black beans, rinsed and drained

½ cup (130 g) refrigerated salsa

½ cup (120 ml) water

4 ounces (115 g) restaurant-style corn tortilla chips

3 ounces (85 g) shredded reduced-fat sharp Cheddar cheese

2 cups (200 g) shredded romaine lettuce

½ cup (115 g) 2% plain Greek yogurt

⅛ teaspoon salt

On your pressure cooker, select Sauté/Browning + more to preheat the cooking pot. Once hot, add the turkey, chili powder, and cumin to the pot. Cook until browned, stirring occasionally. Add the black beans, salsa, and water.

Lock the lid in place and close the seal valve. Press the Cancel button. Press the Manual button to set the cook time for 4 minutes. When the cook time ends, use a quick pressure release.

Meanwhile, preheat the broiler.

When the valve drops, carefully remove the lid.

Place the tortilla chips on a baking sheet in a single layer. Using a slotted spoon, remove the turkey mixture from the pot and sprinkle it over the chips.

Press the Cancel button. Select Sauté/Browning + more. Bring the liquid in the pot to a boil. Cook for 5 minutes, or until thickened slightly. Spoon over the turkey and sprinkle with the cheese. Broil for 1 minute, or until the cheese melts. Remove from the broiler. Sprinkle with the lettuce and spoon yogurt over all. Season with salt.

YIELD: Makes 3 cups (780 g) turkey mixture, 4 ounces (112 g) chips, and 2 cups (200 g) lettuce

SERVES 4: 1 ounce (28 g) chips, ¾ cup (195 g) turkey mixture, and ½ cup (50 g) lettuce per serving

Nutrition Facts

SERVING SIZE (195 G)

AMOUNT PER SERVING

Calories: **340**

		% Daily Value
Total Fat	16g	21%
Saturated Fat	5g	25%
Trans Fat	0g	
Cholesterol	60mg	20%
Sodium	520mg	23%
Total Carbohydrate	28g	10%
Dietary Fiber	5g	18%
Total Sugars	2g	
Added Sugars	0g	
Protein	21g	
Vitamin D	0mcg	
Calcium	224mg	15%
Iron	2mg	10%
Potassium	282mg	6%

COTTAGE PIE IN A POT

This is a fun and fast way to make a family favorite . . . upside down! Sauté the turkey mixture in the pot first, then cook and mash the potatoes and finish the dish by topping with the turkey and the cheese . . . all in one pot and waiting to be scooped onto your plate.

Nonstick cooking spray, for preparing the cooking pot

12 ounces (340 g) 93% lean ground turkey

1 zucchini, cut into ½-inch (1 cm) cubes

2 teaspoons chili powder

2 teaspoons light soy sauce

3½ cups (840 ml) water, divided

½ teaspoon salt, divided

¼ teaspoon black pepper, divided

1 pound (454 g) red potatoes, cut into ½-inch (1 cm) cubes

¾ cup (180 ml) nonfat evaporated milk

2 ounces (55 g) shredded reduced-fat sharp Cheddar cheese

On your pressure cooker, select Sauté/Browning + more to preheat the cooking pot. Once hot, coat the pot with cooking spray. Add the ground turkey. Cook for 4 minutes, or until beginning to lightly brown, stirring occasionally. Add the zucchini, chili powder, soy sauce, ½ cup (120 ml) of water, ⅛ teaspoon of salt, and ⅛ teaspoon of pepper. Cook for 2 minutes, or until the zucchini is just crisp-tender. Transfer the mixture to a bowl and cover with aluminum foil to keep warm.

Add the remaining 3 cups (720 ml) of water to the pressure cooker cooking pot and place a steamer basket inside the pot. Place the potatoes in the steamer basket.

Lock the lid in place and close the seal valve. Press the Cancel button. Press the Manual button to set the cook time for 5 minutes. When the cook time ends, use a quick pressure release.

Nutrition Facts

SERVING SIZE (308 G)

AMOUNT PER SERVING

Calories: **300**

		% Daily Value
Total Fat	11g	14%
Saturated Fat	4g	20%
Trans Fat	0g	
Cholesterol	75mg	25%
Sodium	650mg	28%
Total Carbohydrate	26g	9%
Dietary Fiber	3g	11%
Total Sugars	8g	
Added Sugars	0g	
Protein	26g	
Vitamin D	1mcg	6%
Calcium	287mg	20%
Iron	2m	10%
Potassium	1,002mg	20%

When the valve drops, carefully remove the lid. Turn off the pressure cooker. Remove the potatoes and steamer basket from the pot. Discard the water and return the potatoes to the pot. Using a potato masher or handheld electric mixer, mash the potatoes in the pot. Add the evaporated milk and mash until well blended. (They may be a little thick at this point.) Season with the remaining ⅜ teaspoon of salt and ⅛ teaspoon of pepper. Spoon the turkey mixture and any accumulated juices evenly over the potatoes. Sprinkle with the cheese.

Select Sauté/Browning + more. Cook, uncovered, for 2 to 3 minutes, or until the mixture *just* comes to a boil around the outer edges of the potatoes. Immediately turn off the pressure cooker and, wearing oven mitts, transfer the cooking pot to a heatproof surface. Let rest for 5 minutes, uncovered, to let the cheese melt and thicken slightly.

YIELD: Makes 6 cups (1.8 kg)

SERVES 4: 1½ cups (450 g) per serving

SAUSAGE PEPPER
PASTA POT

All-in-one-pot dishes are so nice for a variety of reasons, but especially because they only use one vessel to wash later. In this recipe, the ingredients provide a lot of the seasonings within themselves, such as the sausage, the spaghetti sauce, and the olives!

Nonstick cooking spray, for preparing the cooking pot

8 ounces (225 g) Italian turkey sausage

2 large green bell peppers, cut into 1-inch (2.5 cm) pieces

4 ounces (115 g) sliced mushrooms

4 ounces (115 g) multigrain penne (such as Barilla Plus)

1 cup (250 g) prepared reduced-sodium spaghetti sauce

1 cup (240 ml) water

1 tablespoon (2 g) dried basil

⅛ teaspoon red pepper flakes (optional)

2 cups (60 g) fresh baby spinach

16 pitted Kalamata olives, coarsely chopped

1 tablespoon (15 ml) extra-virgin olive oil

On your pressure cooker, select Sauté/Browning + more to preheat the cooking pot. Once hot, coat the pot with cooking spray. Add the sausage. Cook for 4 minutes, or until beginning to brown, stirring occasionally. Stir in the green bell peppers, mushrooms, pasta, spaghetti sauce, water, basil, and red pepper flakes (if using).

Lock the lid in place and close the seal valve. Press the Cancel button. Press the Manual button to set the cook time for 5 minutes. When the cook time ends, use a quick pressure release.

When the valve drops, carefully remove the lid. Add the spinach and olives. Stir for about 1 minute until the spinach is just wilted. Drizzle in the olive oil. Let stand, uncovered, for 2 minutes to thicken slightly and so the flavors blend.

YIELD: Makes 6 cups (1.2 kg)

SERVES 4: 1½ cups (300 g) per serving

Nutrition Facts

SERVING SIZE (300 G)

AMOUNT PER SERVING

Calories: **320**

		% Daily Value
Total Fat	15g	19%
Saturated Fat	2g	10%
Trans Fat	0g	
Cholesterol	30mg	10%
Sodium	800mg	35%
Total Carbohydrate	32g	12%
Dietary Fiber	2g	7%
Total Sugars	8g	
Added Sugars	0g	
Protein	17g	
Vitamin D	0mcg	
Calcium	65mg	6%
Iron	3mg	15%
Potassium	410mg	8%

LOUISIANA SAUSAGE AND PEPPER "DIRTY" RICE

Dirty rice was created in the Creole tradition. When finely chopped ingredients such as sausage, bell pepper, and onion are cooked with white rice, the rice is no longer white, but a bit "murky" in color. Fresh parsley and bright red bell pepper perk up the colors and give layers of flavors to the dish!

Nonstick cooking spray, for preparing the cooking pot

1 (3-ounce, or 85 g) pork andouille sausage link (such as Aidells), finely chopped

8 ounces (225 g) lean ground beef

½ cup (75 g) finely chopped green bell pepper

½ cup (75 g) finely chopped red bell pepper

½ cup (50 g) finely chopped scallion, white and green parts

1 cup (185 g) long-grain white rice, rinsed

1¼ cups (300 ml) water

2 teaspoons seafood seasoning (such as Old Bay)

¼ cup (15 g) chopped fresh parsley

On your pressure cooker, select Sauté/Browning + more to preheat the cooking pot. Once hot, coat the pot with cooking spray. Add the sausage and ground beef. Cook for 3 minutes, or until beginning to lightly brown, stirring frequently. Stir in the green and red bell peppers, scallion, rice, water, and seafood seasoning.

Lock the lid in place and close the seal valve. Press the Cancel button. Press the Manual button to set the cook time for 3 minutes. When the cook time ends, use a natural pressure release.

When the valve drops, carefully remove the lid. Stir in the parsley.

YIELD: Make 4 cups (1.1 kg)

SERVES 4: 1 cup (275 g) per serving

Nutrition Facts		
SERVING SIZE (275 G)		
AMOUNT PER SERVING		
Calories:	**320**	
		% Daily Value
Total Fat	7g	9%
Saturated Fat	3g	15%
Trans Fat	0g	
Cholesterol	50mg	17%
Sodium	660mg	29%
Total Carbohydrate	44g	16%
Dietary Fiber	2g	7%
Total Sugars	2g	
Added Sugars	0g	
Protein	20g	
Vitamin D	0mcg	
Calcium	33mg	2%
Iron	2mg	10%
Potassium	178mg	4%

BURGUNDY BEEF WITH SWEET POTATO MASH

A definite showstopper! Tender beef cooked in red wine and spooned over bright orange mashed sweet potatoes. Perfect by candlelight . . . or not!

Nonstick cooking spray, for preparing the cooking pot

1 pound (454 g) boneless beef chuck, cut into 1-inch (2.5 cm) cubes

2 (0.14-ounce, or 4 g) packets sodium-free beef bouillon granules

1 (8-ounce, or 225 g) can tomato sauce

⅓ cup (80 ml) dry red wine

¼ cup (60 ml) water

1½ cups (225 g) chopped red bell pepper

¾ cup (120 g) chopped onion

1 bay leaf

½ teaspoon garlic powder

½ teaspoon black pepper

½ teaspoon sugar

¼ teaspoon red pepper flakes

1 (24-ounce, or 680 g) package mashed sweet potatoes (such as Simply Potatoes)

On your pressure cooker, select Sauté/Browning + more to preheat the cooking pot. Once hot, coat the pot with cooking spray. Add half the beef. Cook for 5 minutes, *without stirring.*

Add the remaining half of the beef and the bouillon granules, tomato sauce, red wine, water, red bell pepper, onion, bay leaf, garlic powder, black pepper, sugar, and red pepper flakes. Stir to blend.

Lock the lid in place and close the seal valve. Press the Cancel button. Press the Manual button to set the cook time for 30 minutes. When the cook time ends, use a natural pressure release.

When the valve drops, carefully remove the lid. Using a slotted spoon, transfer the beef to a plate.

Press the Cancel button. Select Sauté/Browning + more. Bring the liquid in the pot to a boil. Cook for 7 minutes, or until reduced to 1½ cups (360 ml). Return the beef to the pot and cook for 1 minute to heat through.

Meanwhile, prepare the sweet potatoes according to the package directions. Serve the beef and sauce over the sweet potatoes.

YIELD: Makes 4 cups (1.1 kg) beef mixture and about 2 cups (496 g) mashed sweet potatoes

SERVES 4: 1 cup (276 g) beef mixture and about ½ cup (124 g) sweet potatoes per serving

Nutrition Facts

SERVING SIZE (400 G)

AMOUNT PER SERVING

Calories: **350**

		% Daily Value
Total Fat	6g	8%
Saturated Fat	1.5g	8%
Trans Fat	0g	
Cholesterol	45mg	15%
Sodium	650mg	28%
Total Carbohydrate	42g	15%
Dietary Fiber	3g	11%
Total Sugars	25g	
Added Sugars	1g	2%
Protein	26g	
Vitamin D	0mcg	
Calcium	108mg	8%
Iron	4mg	20%
Potassium	365mg	8%

MEATBALLS AND CREAMY GRAVY

Take a break from traditional spaghetti and meatballs and serve these tender, brown gravy–smothered meatballs as is or over mashed potatoes, rice, or egg noodles. Adding a bit of instant coffee granules to the sauce gives it a beefier flavor!

FOR MEATBALLS:

½ cup (50 g) finely chopped scallion, white and green parts, divided

1 pound (454 g) 93% lean ground turkey

½ cup (78 g) oats

1 large egg

2 teaspoons Dijon mustard

½ teaspoon dried thyme

⅛ teaspoon salt

¼ teaspoon black pepper

Nonstick cooking spray, for preparing the cooking pot

2 teaspoons canola oil, divided

FOR GRAVY:

1 (0.14-ounce, or 4 g) packet sodium-free beef bouillon granulates

1½ teaspoons instant coffee granules

¼ teaspoon salt

1 cup (240 ml) water

2 teaspoons cornstarch

½ cup (120 ml) 2% milk

Black pepper, for seasoning

TO MAKE THE MEATBALLS: Measure 2 tablespoons (12.5 g) of scallion and set aside. In a medium bowl, combine the turkey, remaining scallion, oats, egg, mustard, thyme, salt, and pepper. Mix thoroughly. Shape the meat mixture into 32 small (about 1-inch, or 2.5 cm) balls.

On your pressure cooker, select Sauté/Browning + more to preheat the cooking pot. Once hot, coat the pot with cooking spray. Add 1 teaspoon of canola oil and tilt the pot to coat the bottom lightly. Add half the meatballs. Cook for 2 minutes, *without turning*. Using a fork and spoon, gently turn the meatballs and cook for 3 minutes more, turning occasionally. Remove from the pot and set aside. Repeat with the remaining 1 teaspoon of canola oil and meatballs.

Return all the meatballs to the pot.

TO MAKE THE GRAVY: Sprinkle the meatballs with the bouillon granules, coffee granules, and salt. Pour the water over everything.

Lock the lid in place and close the seal valve. Press Cancel button. Press the Manual button to set the cook time for 10 minutes. When the cook time ends, use a natural pressure release.

Nutrition Facts

SERVING SIZE (183 G)

AMOUNT PER SERVING

Calories: **200**

		% Daily Value
Total Fat	4g	5%
Saturated Fat	1g	5%
Trans Fat	0g	
Cholesterol	95mg	32%
Sodium	380mg	17%
Total Carbohydrate	11g	4%
Dietary Fiber	1g	4%
Total Sugars	2g	
Added Sugars	0g	
Protein	32g	
Vitamin D	1mcg	6%
Calcium	58mg	4%
Iron	2mg	10%
Potassium	131mg	2%

When the valve drops, carefully remove the lid. Using a slotted spoon, transfer the meatballs to a plate and cover to keep warm.

Press the Cancel button. Select Sauté/Browning + more. In a small bowl, stir together the cornstarch and milk, stirring until the cornstarch dissolves. Stir this slurry into the liquid in the pot. Bring to a boil. Cook for 1 to 2 minutes, or until beginning to turn golden and thicken slightly, stirring constantly. Spoon the gravy over the meatballs. Season with pepper and garnish with the reserved scallion.

YIELD: Makes 32 meatballs and ½ cup (120 ml) gravy

SERVES 4: 8 meatballs plus 2 tablespoons (30 ml) gravy per serving

ANDOUILLE SAUSAGE AND RED POTATOES

Smaller andouille sausage links can be found in the meat aisle on hanging racks. They have a slight assertiveness unlike traditional sausage links. Look for andouille varieties that are lower in fat.

Nonstick cooking spray, for preparing the cooking pot

2 (3-ounce, or 85 g) andouille pork sausage links (such as Aidells Cajun), cut into ½-inch (1 cm) cubes

2 cups (480 ml) water

1½ pounds (681 g) red potatoes, coarsely chopped (about ¾-inch, or 2 cm, cubes)

1 cup (150 g) chopped red bell pepper

1 garlic clove, minced

1½ tablespoons (23 ml) extra-virgin olive oil

½ teaspoon dried dill

¼ teaspoon dried thyme

½ teaspoon salt

⅛ teaspoon black pepper

On your pressure cooker, select Sauté/Browning + more to preheat the cooking pot. Once hot, coat the pot with cooking spray. Add the sausage. Cook for 5 minutes, or until browned, stirring occasionally. Remove from the pot and set aside.

Put a steamer basket into the cooking pot and pour in the water. Place the potatoes and red bell pepper into the basket.

Lock the lid in place and close the seal valve. Press the Cancel button. Press the Manual button to set the cook time for 4 minutes. When the cook time ends, use a quick pressure release.

When the valve drops, carefully remove the lid. Transfer the potatoes and peppers to a shallow pan, such as a baking pan. Top with the sausage and remaining ingredients. Toss gently. Cover and let stand for 10 minutes to absorb the flavors and release the natural juices.

YIELD: Makes 6 cups (1.15 kg) total

SERVES 4: 1½ cups (289 g) per serving

Nutrition Facts

SERVING SIZE (289 G)

AMOUNT PER SERVING

Calories: 270

		% Daily Value
Total Fat	11g	14%
Saturated Fat	3g	15%
Trans Fat	0g	
Cholesterol	25mg	8%
Sodium	620mg	27%
Total Carbohydrate	32g	12%
Dietary Fiber	4g	14%
Total Sugars	6g	
Added Sugars	0g	
Protein	11g	
Vitamin D	0mcg	
Calcium	26mg	2%
Iron	2mg	10%
Potassium	914mg	20%

MADEIRA SHORT RIBS

You can skip the browning step in this recipe. Just a 30-second sizzle of the onions and garlic is all that's needed before adding the beef!

1 teaspoon canola oil

3 scallions, white and green parts, chopped, divided

2 garlic cloves, minced

4 bone-in beef short ribs (1½ pounds, or 681 g, total), trimmed

⅓ cup (80 ml) water

3 tablespoons (45 ml) light soy sauce

⅓ cup (80 ml) Madeira wine or dry sherry

1 teaspoon Worcestershire sauce

2 (12-ounce, or 340 g) packages frozen cauliflower rice (such as Green Giant brand)

On your pressure cooker, select Sauté/Browning + more to preheat the cooking pot. Once hot, add the canola oil and tilt the pot to coat the bottom lightly. Measure ¼ cup (25 g) of scallion and set aside. Add the remaining scallion and garlic to the pot. Cook for 30 seconds, stirring constantly. Add the short ribs, water, soy sauce, Madeira, and Worcestershire sauce. Stir to combine.

Lock the lid in place and close the seal valve. Press the Cancel button. Press the Manual button to set the cook time for 45 minutes. When the cook time ends, use a natural pressure release for 15 minutes, then a quick pressure release.

When the valve drops, carefully remove the lid. Transfer the ribs to a plate and cover to keep warm.

Cook the cauliflower rice according to package directions.

Pour the liquid from the cooking pot into a fat separator or measuring cup. Let stand so the fat rises to the top. Skim off the fat and return the liquid to the pot.

Press the Cancel button. Select Sauté/Browning + more. Bring the liquid to a boil. Cook for 3 minutes, or until reduced slightly. Spoon the sauce over the beef and cauliflower. Sprinkle with the reserved scallion.

YIELD: Makes 4 ribs, ½ cup (120 ml) sauce, and about 4 cups (340 g) cauliflower rice total

SERVES 4: 1 rib, 2 tablespoons (30 ml) sauce, and about 1 cup (85 g) cauliflower rice per serving

Nutrition Facts
SERVING SIZE (176 G)

AMOUNT PER SERVING
Calories: 270

		% Daily Value
Total Fat	8g	10%
Saturated Fat	3g	15%
Trans Fat	0g	
Cholesterol	40mg	13%
Sodium	570mg	25%
Total Carbohydrate	22g	8%
Dietary Fiber	1g	4%
Total Sugars	2g	
Added Sugars	0g	
Protein	17g	
Vitamin D	0mcg	
Calcium	17mg	2%
Iron	2mg	10%
Potassium	350mg	8%

BEEF AND MUSHROOM STROGANOFF

There's a neat "trick" to this recipe. You only brown half the beef, quickly reduce any pan juices to the point of browning, and cook the onion a couple of minutes. This method adds to the deep concentrated flavors you'll get in this easy pressure cooker recipe without standing over the pot . . . waiting for the beef to brown in batches!

2 teaspoons canola oil

1 pound (454 g) boneless bottom round beef, trimmed of fat, thinly sliced

1 cup (160 g) chopped onion

8 ounces (225 g) sliced mushrooms

½ cup (120 ml) water

½ cup (120 ml) white wine

2 (0.14-ounce, or 4 g) packets sodium-free beef bouillon granules

2 teaspoons Worcestershire sauce

2 teaspoons ketchup

½ teaspoon garlic powder

3 ounces (85 g) no-yolk egg noodles

1½ ounces (43 g) reduced-fat cream cheese, cut into small cubes

2 teaspoons Dijon mustard

1 teaspoon dried dill

½ teaspoon salt

On your pressure cooker, select Sauté/Browning + more to preheat the cooking pot. Once hot, add the canola oil and tilt the pot to coat the bottom lightly. Add half the beef. Cook for 5 minutes, *without stirring*. With a slotted spoon, transfer the beef to a plate and set aside.

Bring the pan drippings to a boil. Cook for 1 minute, or until the liquid is almost evaporated. Add the onion. Cook for 2 minutes, stirring frequently. Stir in the remaining uncooked beef, browned beef, mushrooms, water, white wine, bouillon granules, Worcestershire sauce, ketchup, and garlic powder.

Lock the lid in place and close the seal valve. Press the Cancel button. Press the Manual button to set the cook time for 15 minutes. When the cook time ends, use a natural pressure release.

When the valve drops, carefully remove the lid.

Nutrition Facts

SERVING SIZE (248 G)

AMOUNT PER SERVING

Calories: **320**

		% Daily Value
Total Fat	11g	14%
Saturated Fat	3.5g	18%
Trans Fat	0g	
Cholesterol	75mg	25%
Sodium	470mg	20%
Total Carbohydrate	23g	8%
Dietary Fiber	1g	4%
Total Sugars	4g	
Added Sugars	0g	
Protein	30g	
Vitamin D	0mcg	
Calcium	47mg	4%
Iron	4mg	20%
Potassium	742mg	15%

Press the Cancel button. Select Sauté/Browning + more. Bring the mixture to a boil. Stir in the noodles. Return the mixture to a boil and cook, uncovered, for 6 minutes, or until the noodles are cooked, stirring occasionally. Turn off the pressure cooker.

In a medium bowl, combine the cream cheese, mustard, dill, salt, and ½ cup (40 g) of the hot noodle mixture. Stir until well blended. Stir this mixture into the beef and noodle mixture in the pot until well combined.

YIELD: Makes 5⅓ cups (1.1 kg) total

SERVES 4: About 1⅓ cups (274 g) per serving

Cook's Note

Adding a small amount of the hot noodle mixture to the cream cheese allows the cheese to melt and prevents the cheese from curdling. This is called "tempering."

FALL-APART POT ROAST AND VEGETABLES

Browning the flour initially gives the gravy a deep, rich flavor. It ties the whole dish together, giving it that home-cooked taste (but without the added fat grams!). If you want to skip the browning, you can, but the gravy will have a much lighter flavor.

---

3 tablespoons (24 g) all-purpose flour

1 tablespoon (15 ml) canola oil

2 pounds (908 g) lean boneless beef chuck roast, about 2½ inches (6 cm) thick, trimmed of fat, patted dry with paper towels

2 cups (182 g) frozen pepper stir-fry

2 celery stalks, cut into 2-inch (5 cm) pieces

1⅓ cups (320 ml) water, divided

1 bay leaf

2 tablespoons (30 g) ketchup

2 (0.14-ounce, or 4 g) packets sodium-free beef bouillon granules

1 teaspoon instant coffee granules

1¼ teaspoons salt, divided

½ teaspoon black pepper, divided

1½ pounds (679 g) petite potatoes, halved

1½ pounds (679 g) carrots, cut into 2-inch (5 cm) pieces

On your pressure cooker, select Sauté/Browning + more to preheat the cooking pot. Once hot, add the flour to the pot. Cook for 10 minutes, or until pale brown, stirring occasionally. Transfer to a plate and set aside.

Add the canola oil to the pot and tilt the pot to coat the bottom lightly. Add the beef. Cook for 5 minutes, *without turning*, to brown one side. Transfer to another plate and set aside.

Add the frozen stir-fry mix, celery, 1 cup (240 ml) of water, and the bay leaf to the pot. Top with the beef (browned-side up). Spread the ketchup over the beef. Sprinkle it with the bouillon granules, coffee granules, 1 teaspoon of salt, and ¼ teaspoon of pepper.

Lock the lid in place and close the seal valve. Press the Cancel button. Press the Manual button to set the cook time for 1 hour, 15 minutes. When the cook time ends, use a quick pressure release.

When the valve drops, carefully remove the lid. Transfer the beef to a serving platter. Cover with aluminum foil to keep warm.

Add the potatoes and carrots to the pot.

(continued)

Nutrition Facts		
SERVING SIZE (368 G)		
AMOUNT PER SERVING		
Calories:	**350**	
	% Daily Value	
Total Fat	9g	12%
Saturated Fat	2.5g	13%
Trans Fat	0g	
Cholesterol	80mg	27%
Sodium	700mg	30%
Total Carbohydrate	36g	13%
Dietary Fiber	6g	21%
Total Sugars	10g	
Added Sugars	1g	2%
Protein	31g	
Vitamin D	0mcg	
Calcium	71mg	6%
Iron	4mg	20%
Potassium	1,157mg	25%

Lock the lid in place and close the seal valve. Press the Cancel button. Press the Manual button to set the cook time for 4 minutes. When the cook time ends, use a quick pressure release. Using a slotted spoon, transfer the vegetables to the platter with the beef, surrounding the beef. Re-cover to keep warm.

In a small bowl, whisk the remaining ⅓ cup (80 ml) of water and the toasted flour until blended. Remove ½ cup (120 ml) of hot liquid from the pot and whisk it into the flour-water mixture until well blended. Add this slurry to the pot along with the remaining ¼ teaspoon of salt and ¼ teaspoon of pepper.

Press the Cancel button. Select Sauté/Browning + more. Bring the liquid to a boil. Boil for 5 minutes, or until reduced to 1½ cups (360 ml).

YIELD: Makes 1 pound (454 g) cooked beef, 9 cups (1.3 kg) vegetables, and 1½ cups (360 ml) gravy

SERVES 6: About 3 ounces (85 g) cooked beef, 1½ cups (223 g) vegetables, and ¼ cup (60 ml) gravy per serving

SMASHED "BAKED" POTATOES WITH SALAMI AND CHEESE

Don't just "fluff" your "baked" potatoes. Fluff, then gently smash 'em with a fork . . . it helps spread out the flavors of the other ingredients; it also makes it look like a really big serving . . . and it's fun to do!

2 cups (480 ml) water

4 (8-ounce, or 225 g) Russet potatoes, scrubbed, wrapped individually in aluminum foil

3 ounces (85 g) shredded reduced-fat sharp Cheddar cheese

1 ounce (28 g) crumbled reduced-fat blue cheese

½ cup (50 g) finely chopped scallion, white and green parts

4 slices hard salami, finely chopped (about 1½ ounces, or 42 g, total)

Pinch cayenne pepper (optional)

¼ teaspoon salt

¼ teaspoon black pepper

Put a trivet into your pressure cooker cooking pot and pour in the water. Place the potatoes on the trivet.

Lock the lid in place and close the seal valve. Press the Manual button to set the cook time for 18 minutes.

Meanwhile, in a medium bowl, combine the Cheddar cheese, blue cheese, scallion, salami, and cayenne (if using). Toss gently to combine and set aside.

When the cook time ends, use a natural pressure release.

When the valve drops, carefully remove the lid. Using tongs or a fork, carefully remove the potatoes.

Turn on the broiler. Split each potato *almost* in half and place them on a baking sheet. Using a fork, fluff the potato (fluffing down to the bottom without tearing the potato skin). Season with salt and pepper. Spoon equal amounts of the cheese mixture on top of each potato, covering the surface. Broil 2 minutes, or until the cheese has melted slightly.

YIELD: Makes 4 stuffed potatoes total

SERVES 4: 1 potato per serving

Nutrition Facts

SERVING SIZE (277 G)

AMOUNT PER SERVING

Calories: **300**

		% Daily Value
Total Fat	9g	12%
Saturated Fat	4.5g	23%
Trans Fat	0g	
Cholesterol	30mg	10%
Sodium	620mg	27%
Total Carbohydrate	43g	16%
Dietary Fiber	3g	11%
Total Sugars	2g	
Added Sugars	0g	
Protein	14g	
Vitamin D	0mcg	
Calcium	230mg	20%
Iron	2mg	10%
Potassium	1,013mg	20%

PORK ROAST WITH ROOT VEGETABLES AU JUS

This is the ideal meal for when the weather turns chilly. It fills you up and fills your kitchen with a heady aroma!

1½ teaspoons paprika

1 teaspoon poultry seasoning

1 teaspoon garlic powder

½ teaspoon black pepper

½ teaspoon salt, divided

⅛ teaspoon cayenne pepper

Nonstick cooking spray, for preparing the cooking pot

1 teaspoon canola oil

1 (2-pound, or 908 g) lean boneless Boston butt pork roast, trimmed of fat (see Cook's Note)

2 large leeks, rinsed well, white and light green portions thinly sliced

1½ cups (360 ml) fat-free reduced-sodium chicken broth

1 pound (454 g) sweet potatoes, peeled and cut into 1-inch (2.5 cm) cubes

8 ounces (225 g) parsnips, peeled and cut into 1-inch (2.5 cm) cubes

In a small bowl, stir together the paprika, poultry seasoning, garlic powder, black pepper, ¼ teaspoon of salt, and the cayenne. Rub the pork all over with the paprika mixture.

On your pressure cooker, select Sauté/Browning + more to preheat the cooking pot. Once hot, coat the pot with cooking spray. Add the canola oil and tilt the pot to coat the bottom lightly. Add the pork. Cook for about 10 minutes, turning to brown on all sides. Remove the pork from the pot and set aside.

Add the leeks to the pot. Cook for 2 minutes. Add the chicken broth and bring to a boil, scraping up any browned bits from the bottom of the pot. Top with the pork.

Lock the lid in place and close the seal valve. Press the Cancel button. Press the Manual button to set the cook time for 50 minutes. When the cook time ends, use a quick pressure release.

When the valve drops, carefully remove the lid. Stir in the sweet potatoes and parsnips.

Lock the lid in place and close the seal valve. Press the Cancel button. Press the Manual button to set the cook time for 5 minutes. When the cook time ends, use a quick pressure release.

(continued)

Nutrition Facts		
SERVING SIZE (423 G)		
AMOUNT PER SERVING		
Calories:	**350**	
	% Daily Value	
Total Fat	9g	12%
Saturated Fat	3g	15%
Trans Fat	0g	
Cholesterol	80mg	27%
Sodium	660mg	29%
Total Carbohydrate	37g	13%
Dietary Fiber	6g	21%
Total Sugars	9g	
Added Sugars	0g	
Protein	29g	
Vitamin D	1mcg	6%
Calcium	102mg	8%
Iron	4mg	20%
Potassium	1,145mg	25%

Transfer the pork to a cutting board and let rest for 15 minutes before slicing. Using a slotted spoon, remove the vegetables and place them in a bowl. Cover with aluminum foil to keep warm.

Press the Cancel button. Select Sauté/Browning + more. Bring the liquid to a boil. Boil for 6 to 8 minutes, or until reduced to 1 cup (240 ml). Stir in the remaining ¼ teaspoon of salt.

YIELD: Makes about 1 pound, 3 ounces (539 g) cooked pork, 6 cups (932 g) vegetables, and 1 cup (240 ml) au jus

SERVES 4: About 4½ ounces (130 g) cooked pork, 1½ cups (233 g) vegetables, and ¼ cup (60 ml) au jus per serving

Cook's Note

When purchasing pork roast, always buy at least 8 ounces (225 g) more than the recipe calls for. No matter how lean it looks . . . there's always more to trim!

SMOKY BACON AND PORK GOULASH ON RICE

The highly flavored bacon, smoked paprika, and red wine are the key ingredients here. When reduced, they create a super, *super* rich sauce! Try it over 2 cups of cooked grits for an interesting change!

4 bacon slices, chopped

1 pound (454 g) pork shoulder blade steak, trimmed of fat and cut into 1-inch (2.5 cm) pieces

1 cup (160 g) finely chopped onions

4 ounces (115 g) sliced baby portobello mushrooms

1 (14.5-ounce, or 410 g) can stewed tomatoes

½ cup (120 ml) red wine

1 tablespoon (8 g) smoked paprika

2 teaspoons light soy sauce

2 (0.14-ounce, or 4 g) packets sodium-free beef bouillon granules

½ teaspoon dried oregano

¼ teaspoon black pepper

¼ teaspoon salt

1 (8.8-ounce, or 250 g) pouch brown rice (such as Uncle Ben's Ready Rice)

On your pressure cooker, select Sauté/Browning + more to preheat the cooking pot. Once hot, add the bacon to the pot. Cook for 5 minutes until crisp, stirring frequently. Transfer to paper towels to drain. Discard the bacon grease. Place the pork in the pot. Add the bacon and remaining ingredients, except the rice.

Lock the lid in place and close the seal valve. Press the Cancel button. Press the Manual button to set the cook time for 25 minutes. When the cook time ends, use a natural pressure release.

When the valve drops, carefully remove the lid. Using a slotted spoon, transfer the meat to a bowl.

Press the Cancel button. Select Sauté/Browning + more. Bring the liquid in the pot to a boil. Cook for 10 minutes, uncovered, or until reduced to 1 cup (240 ml).

Cook the rice according to the package directions. Serve the pork and sauce over the rice.

YIELD: Makes 4 cups (400 g) meat mixture, about 2 cups (250 g) rice, and 1 cup (240 ml) sauce

SERVES 4: 1 cup (100 g) meat mixture, ½ cup (70 g) rice, and ¼ cup (60 ml) sauce per serving

Nutrition Facts

SERVING SIZE (375 G)

AMOUNT PER SERVING

Calories: **250**

		% Daily Value
Total Fat	6g	8%
Saturated Fat	2g	10%
Trans Fat	0g	
Cholesterol	45mg	15%
Sodium	650mg	28%
Total Carbohydrate	25g	9%
Dietary Fiber	2g	7%
Total Sugars	5g	
Added Sugars	0g	
Protein	19g	
Vitamin D	1mcg	6%
Calcium	38mg	2%
Iron	2mg	10%
Potassium	713mg	15%

PUB-STYLE BEEF AND NOODLES

When buying chuck roast, always buy more than needed for the recipe. Even with lean cuts, there's still a bit of fat to be discarded.

2 teaspoons canola oil, divided

1 pound (454 g) lean boneless chuck roast, trimmed and cut into 1-inch (2.5 cm) pieces

3 cups (273 g) frozen peppers and onions

½ (8-ounce, or 225 g) package whole mushrooms

1 cup (240 ml) beer, preferably a dark variety

2 teaspoons sodium-free beef bouillon granules

1½ teaspoons dried oregano

½ teaspoon dried thyme

¾ teaspoon salt, divided

⅓ cup (80 g) ketchup

3 to 4 tablespoons (45 to 60 ml) balsamic vinegar

4 ounces (115 g) no-yolk egg noodles

On your pressure cooker, select Sauté/Browning + more to preheat the cooking pot. Once hot, add 1 teaspoon of canola oil and tilt the pot to coat the bottom lightly. Add half the beef. Cook, *without stirring* for 3 minutes. Using a slotted spoon, transfer to a plate and set aside. Repeat with the remaining canola oil and beef. *Do not stir*.

Return all the beef to the pot. Stir in the peppers and onions, mushrooms, beer, bouillon granules, oregano, thyme, and ¼ teaspoon of salt. In a small bowl, whisk the ketchup and vinegar and spoon the sauce evenly over everything. *Do not stir*.

Lock the lid in place and close the seal valve. Press the Cancel button. Press the Manual button to set the cook time for 20 minutes. When the cook time ends, use a quick pressure release.

When the valve drops, carefully remove the lid. Stir in the noodles and the remaining ½ teaspoon of salt.

Nutrition Facts		
SERVING SIZE (285 G)		
AMOUNT PER SERVING		
Calories:	**340**	
		% Daily Value
Total Fat	7g	9%
Saturated Fat	2g	10%
Trans Fat	0g	
Cholesterol	45mg	15%
Sodium	560mg	24%
Total Carbohydrate	37g	13%
Dietary Fiber	0g	
Total Sugars	12g	
Added Sugars	4g	8%
Protein	27g	
Vitamin D	0mcg	
Calcium	31mg	2%
Iron	3mg	15%
Potassium	430mg	10%

Lock the lid in place and close the seal valve. Press the Cancel button. Press the Manual button to set the cook time for 3 minutes. When the cook time ends, use a quick pressure release.

When the valve drops, carefully remove the lid. Let stand, uncovered, for 5 minutes to absorb the liquid and flavors.

YIELD: Makes 6 cups (1.1 kg) total

SERVES 4: 1½ cups (285 g) per serving

Cook's Note

Spooning the ketchup mixture over the top without stirring prevents the dish from burning, which can be caused by the sugar in the ketchup.

SOUPS AND STEWS

Soups and stews bring comfort. But the truly comforting ones usually take a long time to cook. Pressure cooking can provide that long, slow-simmered flavor and oh-so-tender texture in just minutes—and without turning the veggies into mush! Choosing the right cut of meat, poultry, and vegetables and proper timing are key elements . . . easy elements, though!

SOUPS AND STEWS

CREAMY CHIPOTLE CHICKPEA BISQUE

This simple, humble fare will give you that rich warmth and "stick-to-your-ribs" feeling on the coldest of nights. It's a creamy mixture of puréed chickpeas seasoned with a generous amount of onion, garlic, and chipotle.

2 tablespoons (30 ml) canola oil

2 cups (320 g) chopped onion

4 garlic cloves, peeled

6 ounces (170 g) dried chickpeas, rinsed and drained

3 cups (720 ml) reduced-sodium beef broth

½ teaspoon chipotle powder

½ teaspoon salt

¼ tsp black pepper

½ cup (115 g) reduced-fat sour cream

On your pressure cooker, select Sauté/Browning + more to preheat the cooking pot. Once hot, add the canola oil, onion, and garlic to the pot. Cook for 5 minutes, or until beginning to lightly brown. Add the chickpeas, beef broth, and chipotle powder.

Lock the lid in place and close the seal valve. Press the Cancel button. Press the Manual button to set the cook time for 45 minutes. When the cook time ends, use a quick pressure release.

When the valve drops, carefully remove the lid. Season with salt and pepper. Working in batches, place the chickpea mixture in a blender. Secure the lid, holding it firmly in place, and purée until smooth. Serve topped with sour cream.

YIELD: Makes 4 cups (1.25 kg) total

SERVES 4: 1 cup (313 g) per serving

Nutrition Facts
SERVING SIZE (313 G)

AMOUNT PER SERVING

Calories: **300**

		% Daily Value
Total Fat	13g	17%
Saturated Fat	3g	15%
Trans Fat	0g	
Cholesterol	15mg	5%
Sodium	660mg	29%
Total Carbohydrate	37g	1%
Dietary Fiber	9g	32%
Total Sugars	9g	
Added Sugars	0g	
Protein	12g	
Vitamin D	0mcg	
Calcium	106mg	8%
Iron	3mg	15%
Potassium	563mg	10%

HIDDEN VEGGIE TOMATO BISQUE

This simple-looking tomato soup is jam-packed with veggies, such as onion, carrot, and zucchini . . . and, of course, tomatoes. It's like a vegetable garden in every serving!

2 teaspoons canola oil

1½ cups (240 g) diced onion

1 (28-ounce, or 794 g) can crushed tomatoes, undrained

8 ounces (225 g) fresh or frozen sliced carrots

1 zucchini, chopped

1 tablespoon (3 g) dried oregano

1 teaspoon dried fennel

½ teaspoon garlic powder

1¼ cups (300 ml) water

1½ cups (360 ml) half-and-half

1 teaspoon salt

1½ cups (345 g) plain 2% Greek yogurt

On your pressure cooker, select Sauté/Browning + more to preheat the cooking pot. Once hot, add the canola oil and tilt the pot to coat the bottom lightly. Add the onion. Cook for 4 minutes, or until beginning to lightly brown, stirring frequently. Stir in the tomatoes, carrots, zucchini, oregano, fennel, garlic powder, and water.

Lock the lid in place and close the seal valve. Press the Cancel button. Press the Manual button to set the cook time for 20 minutes. When the cook time ends, use a natural pressure release.

When the valve drops, carefully remove the lid. Working in batches, place the soup in a blender. Secure the lid, holding it down firmly, and purée until smooth. Return the soup to the cooking pot. Stir in the half-and-half and salt.

Serve topped with yogurt.

YIELD: Makes 8 cups (2.1 kg) bisque and 1½ cups (345 g) yogurt

SERVES 6: 1⅓ cups (345 g) soup plus ¼ cup (41 g) yogurt per serving

Nutrition Facts

SERVING SIZE (358 G)

AMOUNT PER SERVING

Calories: **210**

		% Daily Value
Total Fat	10g	13%
Saturated Fat	5g	25%
Trans Fat	0g	
Cholesterol	25mg	8%
Sodium	720mg	31%
Total Carbohydrate	23g	8%
Dietary Fiber	5g	18%
Total Sugars	14g	
Added Sugars	0g	
Protein	11g	
Vitamin D	0mcg	
Calcium	194mg	15%
Iron	2mg	10%
Potassium	776mg	15%

CREAMY "ROASTED" POBLANO SOUP

Traditionally, poblano chiles are roasted, steeped under cover, and the skins removed before adding to a dish. But there's no need for all that trouble and effort here. Simply brown the peppers without much stirring to get the "roasted" taste, and the pressure cooker does the rest!

6 poblano peppers (about 1½ pounds, or 681 g), halved and seeded

2 teaspoons canola oil

1 cup (160 g) chopped onion

½ cup (50 g) sliced celery

1 (14-ounce, or 425 ml) can reduced-sodium chicken broth

1 (15-ounce, or 425 g) can no-salt-added cannellini beans, rinsed and drained

½ teaspoon garlic powder

1 cup (240 ml) half-and-half

¾ teaspoon salt

¼ cup (60 g) light sour cream

Thinly slice 6 poblano pepper halves.

On your pressure cooker, select Sauté/Browning + more to preheat the cooking pot. Once hot, add the canola oil and tilt the pot to coat the bottom lightly. Add the sliced peppers and cook for 10 minutes, or until richly brown on the edges, stirring only occasionally. (You are basically "roasting" the pepper strips. The bottom of the pot will be browned as well.) Stir in the onion, celery, chicken broth, cannellini beans, and garlic powder. Top with the remaining pepper halves.

Lock the lid in place and close the seal valve. Press the Cancel button. Press the Manual button to set the cook time for 5 minutes. When the cook time ends, use a natural pressure release.

When the valve drops, carefully remove the lid. Working in batches, transfer the mixture to a blender. Secure the lid, holding it down firmly, and purée until smooth. Return the puréed mixture to the cooking pot.

Stir in the half-and-half and salt. Serve in shallow bowls, topped with sour cream.

YIELD: Makes 6 cups (1.9 kg) soup and ¼ cup (60 g) sour cream

SERVES 4: 1½ cups (472 g) soup plus 1 tablespoon (15 g) sour cream per serving

Nutrition Facts

SERVING SIZE (472 G)

AMOUNT PER SERVING		
Calories:	**260**	
		% Daily Value
Total Fat	10g	13%
Saturated Fat	5g	25%
Trans Fat	0g	
Cholesterol	25mg	8%
Sodium	750mg	33%
Total Carbohydrate	36g	13%
Dietary Fiber	7g	25%
Total Sugars	14g	
Added Sugars	0g	
Protein	1g	
Vitamin D	0mcg	
Calcium	181mg	15%
Iron	3mg	15%
Potassium	997mg	20%

SUMMER SQUASH AND CHEDDAR SOUP

Summer squash (also known as yellow squash or crookneck squash) is an underused vegetable. It's full of nutritional goodness and pairs well with a variety of sauces and other veggies . . . and adds bulk to any dish without overdoing the carbs!

Nonstick cooking spray, for preparing the cooking pot

1½ cups (225 g) chopped green bell pepper

1 pound (454 g) summer squash, coarsely chopped

¾ cup (75 g) chopped scallion, white and green parts, divided

1 cup (165 g) frozen corn

¾ cup (180 ml) water

¼ teaspoon dried thyme

¼ teaspoon red pepper flakes

¼ teaspoon black pepper

¾ cup (180 ml) 2% milk

½ teaspoon salt

4 ounces (115 g) shredded reduced-fat sharp Cheddar cheese

½ cup (115 g) 2% plain Greek yogurt

On your pressure cooker, select Sauté/Browning + more to preheat the cooking pot. Once hot, coat the pot with cooking spray. Add the green bell pepper. Cook for 4 minutes, or until beginning to lightly brown on the edges, stirring frequently.

Add the squash, ½ cup (50 g) of scallion, and the corn, water, thyme, red pepper flakes, and black pepper.

Lock the lid in place and close the seal valve. Press the Cancel button. Press the Manual button to set the cook time for 2 minutes. When the cook time ends, use a quick pressure release.

When the valve drops, carefully remove the lid. Turn off the pressure cooker.

Stir in the milk and salt. Gradually, stir in the Cheddar cheese. Let stand, uncovered, for 10 minutes to thicken slightly and let the cheese melt.

Serve topped with yogurt and sprinkled with the remaining ¼ cup (25 g) of scallion.

YIELD: Makes 4 cups (1.3 kg) soup and ½ cup (115 g) yogurt

SERVES 4: 1 cup (324 g) soup plus 2 tablespoons (30 g) yogurt per serving

Nutrition Facts
SERVING SIZE (324 G)

AMOUNT PER SERVING

Calories: **200**

		% Daily Value
Total Fat	8g	10%
Saturated Fat	5g	25%
Trans Fat	0g	
Cholesterol	30mg	10%
Sodium	510mg	22%
Total Carbohydrate	20g	7%
Dietary Fiber	4g	14%
Total Sugars	10g	
Added Sugars	0g	
Protein	15g	
Vitamin D	1mcg	6%
Calcium	345mg	25%
Iron	1mg	6%
Potassium	554mg	10%

KALAMATA WHITE BEAN BROTH BOWLS

Prepare the topping first because the natural juices of the ingredients will release while standing, adding more flavor and liquid.

FOR TOPPING:

1 cup (180 g) roasted red peppers, chopped

½ cup (20 g) chopped fresh basil or 2 tablespoons (4 g) dried basil

16 pitted Kalamata olives, coarsely chopped

2 ounces (55 g) crumbled reduced-fat feta cheese

1 tablespoon extra-virgin olive oil

FOR BASE:

1 teaspoon extra-virgin olive oil

1½ cups (240 g) chopped onion

4 garlic cloves, minced

8 ounces (225 g) dried navy beans, sorted, rinsed, and drained

3½ cups (840 ml) water

2 teaspoons dried rosemary

1 bay leaf

½ teaspoon salt

TO MAKE THE TOPPING: In a small bowl, stir together all the topping ingredients. Set aside.

TO MAKE THE BASE: On your pressure cooker, select Sauté/Browning + more to preheat the cooking pot. Once hot, add the olive oil and tilt the pot to coat the bottom lightly. Add the onion. Cook for 3 minutes, or until lightly browned. Add the garlic. Cook for 15 seconds, stirring constantly. Add the beans, water, rosemary, and bay leaf.

Lock the lid in place and close the seal valve. Press the Cancel button. Press the Manual button to set the cook time for 25 minutes. When the cook time ends, use a natural pressure release.

When the valve drops, carefully remove the lid. Using a slotted spoon, remove the beans and divide among 4 shallow bowls. Measure and reserve 1⅓ cups (320 ml) of cooking liquid. Add the salt to the reserved liquid. Spoon the liquid evenly over the beans. Top with the pepper-cheese mixture.

YIELD: Makes about 3 cups (546 g) beans, 1⅓ cups (320 ml) broth, 1⅓ cups (133 g) pepper mixture, and ½ cup (55 g) cheese total

SERVES 4: About ¾ cup (136 g) beans, ⅓ cup (80 ml) broth, ⅓ cup (33 g) pepper mixture, and 2 tablespoons (13.75 g) cheese per serving

Nutrition Facts		
SERVING SIZE (189 G)		
AMOUNT PER SERVING		
Calories:	**350**	
		% Daily Value
Total Fat	12g	15%
Saturated Fat	2g	10%
Trans Fat	0g	
Cholesterol	5mg	2%
Sodium	770mg	33%
Total Carbohydrate	45g	16%
Dietary Fiber	10g	36%
Total Sugars	6g	
Added Sugars	0g	
Protein	16g	
Vitamin D	0mcg	
Calcium	143mg	10%
Iron	4mg	20%
Potassium	787mg	15%

FREEZER-TO-POT BROCCOLI, CORN, AND PEPPER SOUP

This is one of those recipes you can always rely on when you're short on time but really want a hot bowl of comfort.

4 cups (624 g) frozen broccoli florets

3 cups (315 g) frozen peppers and onions

2 cups (364 g) frozen mixed vegetables

½ cup (120 ml) water

½ teaspoon dried thyme

1 bay leaf

⅛ teaspoon red pepper flakes

2 cups (480 ml) 2% milk, divided

1 tablespoon (8 g) cornstarch

½ teaspoon salt

¼ teaspoon black pepper

3 ounces (85 g) shredded reduced-fat sharp Cheddar cheese

1½ ounces (43 g) crumbled reduced-fat blue cheese

¼ cup (15 g) chopped fresh parsley

In the pressure cooker cooking pot, combine the frozen broccoli, peppers and onions, mixed vegetables, water, thyme, bay leaf, and red pepper flakes.

Lock the lid in place and close the seal valve. Press the Manual button to set the cook time for 3 minutes. When the cook time ends, use a quick pressure release.

When the valve drops, carefully remove the lid. Press the Cancel button. Select Sauté/Browning + more. In a small bowl, whisk ¼ cup (60 ml) of milk and the cornstarch until the cornstarch dissolves. Stir this slurry into the broccoli mixture along with ¾ cup (180 ml) of milk. Bring to a boil. Boil for 1 minute, stirring constantly.

Turn off the pressure cooker. Stir in the remaining 1 cup (240 ml) of milk, the salt, and the pepper. Gradually stir in the cheeses. Serve topped with the parsley.

YIELD: Makes 6 cups (2 kg) total

SERVES 4: 1½ cups (514 g) per serving

Nutrition Facts

SERVING SIZE (514 G)

AMOUNT PER SERVING

Calories: **270**

		% Daily Value
Total Fat	9g	12%
Saturated Fat	6g	30%
Trans Fat	0g	
Cholesterol	30mg	10%
Sodium	690mg	30%
Total Carbohydrate	27g	10%
Dietary Fiber	6g	21%
Total Sugars	13g	
Added Sugars	0g	
Protein	17g	
Vitamin D	2mcg	10%
Calcium	426mg	35%
Iron	1mg	6%
Potassium	338mg	8%

CLAM CHOWDER WITH BACON

Bacon adds so much flavor to any dish. The "secrets" to using bacon wisely are to drain it well, be in control of the bacon drippings used, and know when to add the cooked bacon for peak seasoning. Here you have it all!

8 bacon slices, chopped

1 cup (100 g) chopped celery

1 cup (100 g) finely chopped scallion, white and green parts, divided

½ cup (120 ml) dry white wine

3 cups (630 g) frozen diced hash browns

1 (8-ounce, or 240 ml) bottle clam juice

1 bay leaf

½ teaspoon dried thyme

⅛ teaspoon red pepper flakes

2 (6.5-ounce, or 185 g) cans chopped clams, drained

1½ cups (360 ml) 2% milk

1 tablespoon (14 g) light butter with canola oil

½ teaspoon salt

¼ teaspoon black pepper

On your pressure cooker, select Sauté/Browning + more to preheat the cooking pot. Once hot, add the bacon to the pot. Cook for 5 minutes, or until beginning to brown, stirring frequently. Using a slotted spoon, transfer the bacon to paper towels to drain. Discard all but 1 tablespoon (15 ml) of the drippings. Add the celery and ¾ cup (75 g) of scallion. Cook for 4 minutes, or until soft.

Add the wine, scraping up any browned bits from the bottom of the pot. Cook for 3 minutes, or until *almost* evaporated. Add the frozen hash browns, clam juice, bay leaf, thyme, and red pepper flakes.

Lock the lid in place and close the seal valve. Press the Cancel button. Press the Manual button to set the cook time for 5 minutes. When the cook time ends, use a quick pressure release.

When the valve drops, carefully remove the lid. Using a potato masher or immersion blender, mash to create a thicker consistency. Crumble the bacon. Stir in the clams, milk, butter, salt, pepper, and crumbled bacon.

Press the Cancel button. Select Sauté/Browning + more. Bring the chowder to a boil. Turn off the pressure cooker. Serve topped with the remaining ¼ cup (25 g) of scallion.

YIELD: Makes 5 cups (1.25 kg) total

SERVES 4: 1¼ cups (319 g) per serving

Nutrition Facts

SERVING SIZE (319 G)

AMOUNT PER SERVING

Calories: 280

		% Daily Value
Total Fat	12g	15%
Saturated Fat	4.5g	23%
Trans Fat	0g	
Cholesterol	55mg	18%
Sodium	650mg	28%
Total Carbohydrate	20g	7%
Dietary Fiber	1g	4%
Total Sugars	5g	
Added Sugars	0g	
Protein	24g	
Vitamin D	1mcg	6%
Calcium	176mg	15%
Iron	3mg	15%
Potassium	831mg	20%

HEARTY CORN, POTATO, AND ONION CHOWDER WITH SHRIMP

Little yellow Yukon gold potatoes are sold in mesh bags in the produce section of major supermarkets, but if they're not available, use the larger version cut into 1-inch (2.5 cm) chunks. Red potatoes may be substituted, but the yellow potatoes add a "buttery" look to the dish.

1 tablespoon (15 ml) canola oil

2 cups (320 g) chopped onion

¾ cup (180 ml) water

8 ounces (225 g) petite Yukon gold potatoes, cut into 1-inch (2.5 cm) chunks

¾ cup (124 g) frozen corn

⅛ teaspoon red pepper flakes (optional)

12 ounces (340 g) fresh or frozen shrimp, peeled and deveined

2 teaspoons seafood seasoning (such as Old Bay)

½ cup (120 ml) 2% milk

⅓ cup (43 g) frozen green peas

2 tablespoons (28 g) light butter with canola oil

¼ teaspoon salt

¼ teaspoon black pepper, or to taste

¼ cup (25 g) chopped scallion

On your pressure cooker, select Sauté/Browning + more to preheat the cooking pot. Once hot, add the canola oil and tilt the pot to coat the bottom lightly. Add the onion. Cook for 4 minutes, or until beginning to turn golden (do not let them become richly browned), stirring frequently. Add the water, potatoes, corn, and red pepper flakes (if using).

Lock the lid in place and close the seal valve. Press the Cancel button. Press the Manual button to set the cook time for 5 minutes. When the cook time ends, use a quick pressure release.

When the valve drops, carefully remove the lid. Press the Cancel button. Select Sauté/Browning + more. Bring the chowder to a boil. Add the shrimp and seafood seasoning. Return the mixture to a boil and cook for 4 minutes, stirring occasionally. Turn off the pressure cooker. Stir in the milk, peas, butter, salt, and pepper. Let stand, uncovered, for 5 minutes to absorb the flavors. Serve topped with the scallion.

YIELD: Makes 5 cups (1.4 kg) total

SERVES 4: 1¼ cups (355 g) per serving

Nutrition Facts

SERVING SIZE (301 G)

AMOUNT PER SERVING

Calories: 230

		% Daily Value
Total Fat	8g	10%
Saturated Fat	2g	10%
Trans Fat	0g	
Cholesterol	110mg	37%
Sodium	660mg	29%
Total Carbohydrate	24g	9%
Dietary Fiber	3g	11%
Total Sugars	6g	
Added Sugars	0g	
Protein	15g	
Vitamin D	0mcg	0%
Calcium	108mg	8%
Iron	1mg	6%
Potassium	472mg	10%

SEAFOOD AND VEGGIE GUMBO STEW

Many gumbos require expensive ingredients, such as crab. But in this recipe, mild tilapia takes on the taste and texture of crab and leaves your wallet intact!

3 tablespoons (23 g) all-purpose flour

¼ cup (60 ml) canola oil

1½ cups (150 g) chopped celery

3 cups (273 g) frozen pepper stir-fry

2 (14.5-ounce, or 410 g) cans stewed tomatoes

2 cups (480 ml) water

1½ tablespoons (11 g) seafood seasoning (such as Old Bay), divided

4 bay leaves

1 teaspoon garlic powder

12 ounces (340 g) frozen tilapia fillets

12 ounces (340 g) frozen peeled and deveined medium shrimp

1 pound (454 g) frozen cut okra

1 tablespoon (15 ml) hot sauce (such as Frank's)

1 teaspoon salt

4 cups cooked brown rice (800 g) or cooked white rice (740 g)

On your pressure cooker, select Sauté/Browning + more to preheat the cooking pot. Once hot, combine the flour and canola oil in the pot. Cook for 10 minutes, stirring constantly with a flat spatula until light brown.

Add the celery. Cook for 3 minutes, stirring frequently. Stir in the frozen pepper stir-fry, tomatoes, water, 1 tablespoon (7 g) of seafood seasoning, the bay leaves, and the garlic powder.

Lock the lid in place and close the seal valve. Press the Cancel button. Press the Manual button to set the cook time for 20 minutes. When the cook time ends, use a natural pressure release.

When the valve drops, carefully remove the lid. Add the tilapia, shrimp, okra, hot sauce, and salt.

Lock the lid in place and close the seal valve. Press the Cancel button. Press the Manual button to set the cook time for 2 minutes. When the cook time ends, use a quick pressure release.

(continued)

Nutrition Facts		
SERVING SIZE (273 G)		
AMOUNT PER SERVING		
Calories:	**220**	
	% Daily Value	
Total Fat	6g	8%
Saturated Fat	0.5g	3%
Trans Fat	0g	
Cholesterol	50mg	17%
Sodium	690mg	30%
Total Carbohydrate	28g	10%
Dietary Fiber	3g	11%
Total Sugars	4g	
Added Sugars	0g	
Protein	13g	
Vitamin D	1mcg	6%
Calcium	82mg	6%
Iron	2mg	10%
Potassium	435mg	10%

When the valve drops, carefully remove the lid. Stir and let stand, uncovered, for 15 minutes to thicken and for the flavors to develop. (Note: The ingredients will continue to cook while standing.) Serve over the rice.

YIELD: Makes 12 cups (2.8 kg) gumbo and 4 cups (800 g) cooked brown rice

SERVES 12: 1 cup (233 g) gumbo plus ⅓ cup (67 g) rice per serving

Cook's Note

This is even better the next day, and leftovers freeze well for up to two months; freeze the gumbo and rice separately. However, it's best to freeze in individual servings, if possible, for easy thawing and portion control. Thaw in the refrigerator overnight and reheat in a covered saucepan over low heat. Timing will vary depending on how much is frozen.

BUFFALO WING CHICKEN CHILI

Chicken thighs, hot sauce, and blue cheese—an ever-popular combination. Use a mild Louisiana hot sauce to bring out the flavors while controlling the heat.

2 tablespoons (30 ml) extra-virgin olive oil, divided

Nonstick cooking spray, for coating the chicken

1½ pounds (681 g) boneless, skinless chicken thighs, trimmed of fat

3 cups (720 ml) reduced-sodium chicken broth

2 (14.5-ounce, or 410 g) cans diced fire-roasted tomatoes

8 garlic cloves, minced

3 tablespoons (45 ml) hot pepper sauce (such as Frank's), divided

1 (8.8-ounce, or 250 g) pouch brown rice (such as Uncle Ben's Ready Rice)

1 ounce (28 g) crumbled reduced-fat blue cheese

On your pressure cooker, select Sauté/Browning + more to preheat the cooking pot. Once hot, add 2 teaspoons of olive oil and tilt the pot to coat the bottom lightly. Coat half the chicken with cooking spray and add it to the pot. Cook for 5 minutes, *without turning*. Turn the chicken and add the uncooked chicken, chicken broth, tomatoes, garlic, and 2 tablespoons (30 ml) of hot sauce.

Lock the lid in place and close the seal valve. Press the Cancel button. Press the Manual button to set the cook time for 8 minutes. When the cook time ends, use a natural pressure release for 5 minutes, then a quick pressure release.

When the valve drops, carefully remove the lid. Using a fork, stir the chili to break up the chicken in the pot. Stir in the remaining 1 tablespoon plus 1 teaspoon (20 ml) of olive oil and 1 tablespoon (15 ml) of hot sauce.

Prepare the rice according to the package directions and divide it among 6 bowls. Top with equal amounts of the chili and sprinkle evenly with the blue cheese.

YIELD: Makes 7 cups (2.1 kg) chicken mixture, about 2 cups (280 g) rice, and ¼ cup (28 g) cheese

SERVES 6: About 1 cup (354 g) chicken mixture, ½ cup (140 g) rice, and 2 teaspoons (4.6 g) blue cheese per serving

Cook's Note
Freeze any remaining chicken, rice, and blue cheese in separate airtight containers or resealable plastic bags. Best if packaged in individual servings for portion control.

Nutrition Facts		
SERVING SIZE (410 G)		
AMOUNT PER SERVING		
Calories:	**340**	
	% Daily Value	
Total Fat	15g	19%
Saturated Fat	4g	20%
Trans Fat	0g	
Cholesterol	80mg	27%
Sodium	790mg	34%
Total Carbohydrate	20g	7%
Dietary Fiber	2g	7%
Total Sugars	5g	
Added Sugars	0g	
Protein	27g	
Vitamin D	0mcg	
Calcium	87mg	6%
Iron	3mg	15%
Potassium	311mg	6%

CHICKEN AND VEGGIE NOODLE SOUP

Be sure to use bone-in chicken thighs. They add more "calorie-free" flavor and the meat is so tender it falls off the bone!

Nonstick cooking spray, for preparing the cooking pot

1 teaspoon canola oil

1 cup (160 g) chopped onion

1 cup (100 g) sliced celery

1 pound (454 g) bone-in skinless chicken thighs, trimmed of fat

1 cup (130 g) fresh or frozen sliced carrots

3 cups (720 ml) reduced-sodium chicken broth

¾ teaspoon poultry seasoning

3 ounces (85 g) no-yolk egg noodles

3 tablespoons (42 g) light butter with canola oil

½ teaspoon salt

¼ teaspoon black pepper

On your pressure cooker, select Sauté/Browning + more to preheat the cooking pot. Once hot, coat the pot with cooking spray. Add the canola oil and tilt the pot to coat the bottom lightly. Add the onion. Cook for 2 minutes. Add the celery. Cook for 1 minute. Add the chicken, carrots, chicken broth, and poultry seasoning.

Lock the lid in place and close the seal valve. Press the Cancel button. Press the Manual button to set the cook time for 15 minutes. When the cook time ends, use a natural pressure release for 5 minutes, then a quick pressure release.

When the valve drops, carefully remove the lid. Using a slotted spoon, transfer the chicken to a plate. Add the noodles to the liquid in the pot.

Lock the lid in place and close the seal valve. Press the Cancel button. Press the Manual button to set the cook time for 3 minutes. When the cook time ends, use a quick pressure release.

Remove the chicken from the bones and coarsely chop the meat. Add the chicken, butter, salt, and pepper to the noodles. Stir to combine.

YIELD: Makes 5 cups (1.5 kg) total

SERVES 4: 1¼ cups (372 g) per serving

Nutrition Facts		
SERVING SIZE (372 G)		
AMOUNT PER SERVING		
Calories:	**280**	
	% Daily Value	
Total Fat	12g	15%
Saturated Fat	3.5g	18%
Trans Fat	0g	
Cholesterol	60mg	20%
Sodium	780mg	34%
Total Carbohydrate	23g	8%
Dietary Fiber	2g	7%
Total Sugars	5g	
Added Sugars	0g	
Protein	20g	
Vitamin D	0mcg	
Calcium	46mg	4%
Iron	2mg	10%
Potassium	316mg	6%

ITALIAN SAUSAGE AND VEGGIE SOUP STEW

This "throw-it-together" hearty soup stew tastes like it's been over a low simmer all day, and it is so satisfying! The hot sausage is a multitasker . . . it adds a certain level of heat, contains multiple herbs for seasoning, and contributes some saltiness!

Nonstick cooking spray, for preparing the cooking pot

3 (3-ounce, or 85 g) hot Italian turkey sausage links, casings removed

1 cup fresh (100 g) or frozen (124 g) cut green beans

1 cup (130 g) fresh or frozen sliced carrots

1 (8-ounce, or 225 g) package sliced mushrooms

1 (14.5-ounce, or 410 g) can diced fire-roasted tomatoes with garlic

1 cup (240 ml) water

¼ teaspoon dried fennel or Italian seasoning

1 medium zucchini, chopped

1 ounce (28 g) Asiago cheese, shredded

On your pressure cooker, select Sauté/Browning + more to preheat the cooking pot. Once hot, coat the pot with cooking spray. Add the sausage. Cook for 4 minutes, stirring frequently. Add the green beans, carrots, mushrooms, tomatoes, water, and fennel.

Lock the lid in place and close the seal valve. Press the Cancel button. Press the Manual button to set the cook time for 15 minutes. When the cook time ends, use a quick pressure release.

When the valve drops, carefully remove the lid. Stir in the zucchini. Press the Cancel button. Select Sauté/Browning + more. Bring the soup stew to a boil. Cook, uncovered, for 3 minutes, or until the zucchini is just crisp-tender.

Top with the cheese before serving.

YIELD: Makes 6 cups (1.3 kg) total

SERVES 4: 1½ cups (332 g) per serving

Cook's Note
For a thinner consistency, add ½ cup (120 ml) water at the end of the cook time.

Nutrition Facts

SERVING SIZE (332 G)

AMOUNT PER SERVING

Calories:	200	
		% Daily Value
Total Fat	10g	13%
Saturated Fat	1.5g	8%
Trans Fat	0g	
Cholesterol	45mg	15%
Sodium	700mg	30%
Total Carbohydrate	13g	5%
Dietary Fiber	5g	18%
Total Sugars	7g	
Added Sugars	0g	
Protein	16g	
Vitamin D	0mcg	
Calcium	120mg	10%
Iron	3mg	15%
Potassium	710mg	15%

PORK SALSA VERDE POZOLE

Some recipes call for rinsing hominy before adding it to a dish, but not here. The heady, musky flavors become blended quickly thanks to the use of the pressure cooker and give the dish a deep corn flavor.

Nonstick cooking spray, for preparing the cooking pot

1 teaspoon canola oil

12 ounces (340 g) boneless pork shoulder, trimmed and cut into ½-inch (1 cm) pieces

1 cup (160 g) chopped onion

2 (15-ounce, or 425 g) cans white hominy, drained

1½ cups (360 ml) water

½ cup (64 g) salsa verde

2 (0.14-ounce, or 4 g) packets sodium-free chicken bouillon granules

2 teaspoons ground cumin, divided

1 teaspoon garlic powder

1 teaspoon Worcestershire sauce

¼ cup (4 g) fresh cilantro leaves

¼ cup (60 g) light sour cream

1 lime, quartered

On your pressure cooker, select Sauté/Browning + more to preheat the cooking pot. Once hot, coat the pot with cooking spray. Add the canola oil and tilt the pot to coat the bottom lightly. Add the pork. Cook for 5 minutes, *without stirring*. Remove from the pot and set aside.

Add the onion to the pot. Cook for 2 minutes, stirring occasionally. Stir in the pork, hominy, water, salsa verde, bouillon granules, 1½ teaspoons of cumin, the garlic powder, and the Worcestershire sauce.

Lock the lid in place and close the seal valve. Press the Cancel button. Press the Manual button to set the cook time for 15 minutes. When the cook time ends, use a quick pressure release.

When the valve drops, carefully remove the lid. Stir in the remaining ½ teaspoon of cumin and the cilantro. Serve topped with sour cream and lime wedges.

YIELD: Makes about 6 cups (1.2 kg) total

SERVES 4: About 1½ cups (289 g) per serving

Nutrition Facts

SERVING SIZE (289 G)

AMOUNT PER SERVING

Calories: 230

		% Daily Value
Total Fat	8g	10%
Saturated Fat	2.5g	13%
Trans Fat	0g	
Cholesterol	35mg	12%
Sodium	780mg	34%
Total Carbohydrate	28g	10%
Dietary Fiber	4g	14%
Total Sugars	8g	
Added Sugars	0g	
Protein	12g	
Vitamin D	0mcg	
Calcium	58mg	4%
Iron	2mg	10%
Potassium	356mg	8%

TACO CHILI BOWLS

This thick and hearty dish is even better the next day and takes on the flavor and texture of tamales.

Nonstick cooking spray, for preparing the cooking pot

12 ounces (340 g) 93% lean ground beef

1 pint (300 g) grape tomatoes

½ (15-ounce, or 425 g) can no-salt-added black beans, rinsed and drained

1 cup (240 ml) water

1 (1-ounce, or 28 g) packet 30% reduced-sodium taco seasoning mix

4 ounces (115 g) corn tortilla chips, crumbled

¼ teaspoon salt

2 teaspoons sugar (optional)

¼ cup (60 g) light sour cream

1 lime, quartered

On your pressure cooker, select Sauté/Browning + more to preheat the cooking pot. Once hot, coat the pot with cooking spray. Add the ground beef. Cook for 3 minutes, or until browned, stirring occasionally. Add the tomatoes, beans, water, and taco seasoning.

Lock the lid in place and close the seal valve. Press the Cancel button. Press the Manual button to set the cook time for 5 minutes. When the cook time ends, use a quick pressure release.

When the valve drops, carefully remove the lid. Stir in the chips, salt, and sugar (if using), breaking up any larger pieces of tomato.

Serve topped with equal amounts of sour cream, with lime wedges for squeezing.

YIELD: Makes 4 cups (984 g) total

SERVES 4: 1 cup (246 g) per serving

Cook's Note

This will be a dense dish. For a thinner consistency, add ½ cup (120 ml) water after the chips have been incorporated.

Nutrition Facts

SERVING SIZE (246 G)

AMOUNT PER SERVING

Calories: 350

		% Daily Value
Total Fat	14g	18%
Saturated Fat	4g	20%
Trans Fat	0g	
Cholesterol	60mg	20%
Sodium	650mg	28%
Total Carbohydrate	34g	12%
Dietary Fiber	3g	11%
Total Sugars	6g	
Added Sugars	0g	
Protein	23g	
Vitamin D	0mcg	
Calcium	82mg	6%
Iron	3mg	15%
Potassium	311mg	6%

BEEF, BARLEY, AND BABY PORTOBELLO STEW

Baby portobello mushrooms have a "meatier" texture than common white button mushrooms, which gives this stew lots of body.

Nonstick cooking spray, for preparing the cooking pot

1 pound (454 g) lean stew meat

1 cup (160 g) chopped onion

½ teaspoon garlic powder

2 tablespoons (32 g) tomato paste

1 (14.5-ounce, or 410 g) can diced fire-roasted tomatoes

2½ cups (600 ml) water

3 (0.14-ounce, or 4 g) packets sodium-free beef bouillon granules

⅔ cup (133 g) pearl barley, rinsed and drained

1 cup (130 g) fresh or frozen sliced carrots

8 ounces (225 g) sliced baby portobello mushrooms or white button mushrooms

1 tablespoon (15 ml) Worcestershire sauce

1 bay leaf

½ teaspoon dried thyme

¼ teaspoon black pepper

1 teaspoon salt

On your pressure cooker, select Sauté/Browning + more to preheat the cooking pot. Once hot, coat the pot with cooking spray. Add the stew meat. Cook for 5 minutes, *without stirring*. Stir in the remaining ingredients, except the salt.

Lock the lid in place and close the seal valve. Press the Cancel button. Press the Manual button to set the cook time for 25 minutes. When the cook time ends, use a natural pressure release for 10 minutes, then a quick pressure release.

When the valve drops, carefully remove the lid. Stir in the salt. Turn off the heat and let stand, uncovered, for 20 minutes to let the flavors absorb.

YIELD: Makes 8 cups (1.4 kg) total

SERVES 6: 1⅓ cups (231 g) per serving

Nutrition Facts
SERVING SIZE (231 G)

AMOUNT PER SERVING

Calories: **240**

		% Daily Value
Total Fat	6g	8%
Saturated Fat	2g	10%
Trans Fat	0g	
Cholesterol	45mg	15%
Sodium	640mg	28%
Total Carbohydrate	28g	10%
Dietary Fiber	6g	2%
Total Sugars	6g	
Added Sugars	0g	
Protein	19g	
Vitamin D	0mcg	
Calcium	39mg	4%
Iron	3mg	15%
Potassium	508mg	10%

BEEF AND PINTO BEAN CHILI STEW

A "throw-and-go" meal with the only one ingredient to chop (the cilantro or scallion).
So simple! So goooood!

Nonstick cooking spray, for preparing the cooking pot

12 ounces (340 g) lean ground beef

4 ounces (115 g) dried pinto beans, rinsed and drained

12 ounces (360 ml) light beer (such as Miller Lite)

1 (10-ounce, or 280 g) can diced tomatoes with lime juice and cilantro

1 (4.5-ounce, or 130 g) can chopped mild green chiles

¾ cup (123.75 g) frozen corn

1 cup (240 ml) water

1 (1-ounce, or 28 g) package 30% reduced-sodium taco seasoning

½ cup chopped fresh cilantro (8 g) or chopped scallion (50 g)

On your pressure cooker, select Sauté/Browning + more to preheat the cooking pot. Once hot, coat the pot with cooking spray. Add the ground beef. Cook for about 3 minutes until browned, stirring frequently. Add the beans, beer, tomatoes, chiles, corn, and water.

Lock the lid in place and close the seal valve. Press the Cancel button. Press the Manual button to set the cook time for 35 minutes. When the cook time ends, use a quick pressure release.

When the valve drops, carefully remove the lid. Stir in the taco seasoning and cilantro (or scallion). Let stand, uncovered, for 10 minutes to absorb the flavors.

YIELD: Makes 5 cups (1.3 kg) total

SERVES 4: 1¼ cups (332 g) per serving

Nutrition Facts
SERVING SIZE (332 G)

AMOUNT PER SERVING
Calories: **310**

		% Daily Value
Total Fat	6g	8%
Saturated Fat	3g	15%
Trans Fat	0g	
Cholesterol	55mg	18%
Sodium	810mg	35%
Total Carbohydrate	34g	12%
Dietary Fiber	8g	29%
Total Sugars	6g	
Added Sugars	0g	
Protein	25g	
Vitamin D	0mcg	
Calcium	63mg	4%
Iron	3mg	15%
Potassium	473mg	10%

VEGETABLE BEEF SOUP

When buying chuck, the purchased weight needs to be about 8 ounces (225 g) more than the recipe calls for. Even lean chuck has to be trimmed. This soup, like most soups, tastes even better the next day.

2 tablespoons (30 ml) extra-virgin olive oil, divided

1½ pounds (679 g) lean boneless beef chuck, trimmed of fat and cut into 1-inch (2.5 cm) cubes

1 (14-ounce, or 397 g) package frozen pepper stir-fry

2 cups fresh (200 g) or frozen (248 g) green beans, cut into 2-inch (5 cm) pieces

1 cup (130 g) fresh or frozen sliced carrots

1 (14.5-ounce, or 410 g) can stewed tomatoes

1 cup (240 ml) water

3 (0.14-ounce, or 4 g) packets sodium-free beef bouillon granules

1 tablespoon (3 g) dried oregano

4 cups (360 g) coarsely chopped green cabbage

3 tablespoons (45 g) ketchup

1 tablespoon (15 ml) Worcestershire sauce

1 teaspoon salt

On your pressure cooker, select Sauté/Browning + more to preheat the cooking pot. Once hot, add 1 tablespoon (15 ml) of olive oil and tilt the pot to coat the bottom lightly. Add half the beef. Cook for 5 minutes, *without stirring*. Stir in the remaining beef and top it with the frozen pepper stir-fry, green beans, carrots, tomatoes, water, bouillon granules, and oregano.

Lock the lid in place and close the seal valve. Press the Cancel button. Press the Manual button to set the cook time for 20 minutes. When the cook time ends, use a quick pressure release.

When the valve drops, carefully remove the lid. Add the cabbage, ketchup, Worcestershire sauce, salt, and remaining 1 tablespoon (15 ml) of olive oil.

Nutrition Facts

SERVING SIZE (321 G)

AMOUNT PER SERVING

Calories: **250**

		% Daily Value
Total Fat	9g	12%
Saturated Fat	2.5g	13%
Trans Fat	0g	
Cholesterol	45mg	15%
Sodium	720mg	31%
Total Carbohydrate	16g	6%
Dietary Fiber	4g	14%
Total Sugars	10g	
Added Sugars	2g	4%
Protein	24g	
Vitamin D	0mcg	
Calcium	69mg	6%
Iron	3mg	15%
Potassium	335mg	8%

Lock the lid in place and close the seal valve. Press the Cancel button. Press the Manual button to set the cook time for 4 minutes. When the cook time ends, use a natural pressure release for 15 minutes, then a quick pressure release.

When the valve drops, carefully remove the lid and serve.

YIELD: Makes about 10 cups (1.9 kg) total

SERVES 6: About 1⅔ cups (321 g) per serving

Cook's Notes

Freeze in individual servings for easy thawing and portion control. Thaw in the refrigerator overnight and reheat in a covered saucepan over low heat. Timing will vary depending on how much is frozen.

CATTLE TRAIL CHILI

The touch of honey doesn't add sweetness here, but acts as a blender providing overall mellowness to the dish. As with most chili, the flavors are even better the next day!

---

1 tablespoon (15 ml) canola oil

1 pound (454 g) 93% fat-free ground turkey

1½ cups (240 g) chopped onion

1 (14.5-ounce, or 410 g) can stewed tomatoes

2 tablespoons (32 g) tomato paste

1 (15-ounce, or 425 g) can no-salt-added dark red kidney beans, drained and rinsed

1 (12-fluid-ounce, or 360 ml) light beer (such as Miller Lite)

3 tablespoons (23 g) chili powder

1½ tablespoons (11 g) ground cumin

2 teaspoons dried oregano

1 teaspoon garlic powder

1 tablespoon (20 g) honey

½ teaspoon salt

½ cup chopped fresh cilantro (8 g) or parsley (30 g)

On your pressure cooker, select Sauté/Browning + more to preheat the cooking pot. Once hot, add the canola oil and tilt the pot to coat the bottom lightly. Add the ground turkey. Cook for 4 minutes, or until browned, stirring occasionally. Add the onion, tomatoes, tomato paste, kidney beans, beer, chili powder, cumin, oregano, and garlic powder.

Lock the lid in place and close the seal valve. Press the Cancel button. Press the Manual button to set the cook time for 15 minutes. When the cook time ends, use a quick pressure release.

Nutrition Facts		
SERVING SIZE (308 G)		
AMOUNT PER SERVING		
Calories:	**260**	
	% Daily Value	
Total Fat	10g	13%
Saturated Fat	2g	10%
Trans Fat	0g	
Cholesterol	55mg	18%
Sodium	570mg	25%
Total Carbohydrate	22g	8%
Dietary Fiber	7g	25%
Total Sugars	7g	
Added Sugars	3g	6%
Protein	19g	
Vitamin D	0mcg	
Calcium	89mg	6%
Iron	3mg	15%
Potassium	526mg	10%

When the valve drops, carefully remove the lid. Stir in the honey, salt, and cilantro.

YIELD: Makes 7 cups (about 2.2 kg) total

SERVES 7: About 1 cup (308 g) per serving

Cook's Notes

Lightly coat the measuring spoon with cooking spray before measuring the honey. It prevents the honey from sticking to the spoon so it releases quickly! It's best to freeze this in individual servings, if possible, for easy thawing and portion control. Thaw in the refrigerator overnight and reheat in a covered saucepan over low heat. Timing will vary depending on how much is frozen.

COCONUT CURRY PORK BOWLS

This is definitely the perfect way to "debone" effortlessly. The pork literally falls off the bones while cooking, so all you have to do is remove them from the pot and give everything a quick stir to break down the larger pieces.

2 cups (182 g) frozen pepper stir-fry

1 (8-ounce, or 225 g) can pineapple tidbits in juice, drained

⅓ cup (50 g) raisins

1 cup (240 ml) reduced-sodium chicken broth, divided

1½ tablespoons (9 g) curry powder

1 teaspoon garlic powder

2 (6-ounce, or 170 g) bone-in pork sirloin chops, trimmed of fat

2 teaspoons roasted red chile paste

1 cup (240 ml) light coconut milk

½ cup (65 g) frozen green peas

2 teaspoons grated peeled fresh ginger

½ teaspoon salt

¼ cup (4 g) chopped fresh cilantro leaves

1 (8.8-ounce, or 250 g) pouch brown rice, (such as Uncle Ben's Ready Rice)

In your pressure cooker cooking pot, combine the frozen pepper stir-fry, pineapple, raisins, ¾ cup (180 ml) of chicken broth, the curry powder, and the garlic powder. Top with the pork chops. In a small bowl, stir together the remaining ¼ cup (60 ml) of broth and the chile paste. Spoon this over the pork.

Lock the lid in place and close the seal valve. Press the Manual button to set the cook time for 18 minutes. When the cook time ends, use a quick pressure release.

When the valve drops, carefully remove the lid. Remove the bones from the pot. Stir in the coconut milk, peas, ginger, salt, and cilantro (stirring the mixture will help break the pork into smaller pieces).

Prepare the rice according to the package directions. Spoon equal amounts of rice into 4 bowls and spoon the pork curry mixture on top.

YIELD: Makes 4 cups (1.2 kg) pork mixture plus about 2 cups (250 g) rice

SERVES 4: 1 cup (308 g) pork mixture plus about ½ cup (63 g) rice per serving

Nutrition Facts

SERVING SIZE (434 G)

AMOUNT PER SERVING

Calories: 330

		% Daily Value
Total Fat	8g	10%
Saturated Fat	5g	25%
Trans Fat	0g	
Cholesterol	40mg	13%
Sodium	550mg	24%
Total Carbohydrate	45g	16%
Dietary Fiber	2g	7%
Total Sugars	15g	
Added Sugars	0g	
Protein	18g	
Vitamin D	0mcg	
Calcium	24mg	2%
Iron	1mg	6%
Potassium	469mg	10%

TARRAGON-HAM HOCK BEAN SOUP

"Hard-day comfort" is the perfect description for this hearty soup. The tarragon is the secret ingredient that sets this old favorite apart.

8 ounces (225 g) dried Great Northern beans, rinsed

2 smoked ham hocks (about 1 pound, or 454 g, total)

1½ cups (150 g) chopped celery

1½ cups (195 g) frozen sliced carrots

1½ cups (240 g) chopped onion

1 bay leaf

½ to 1 teaspoon dried tarragon

4 cups (960 ml) water

¾ teaspoon salt

In your pressure cooker cooking pot, combine everything except the salt.

Lock the lid in place and close the seal valve. Press the Manual button to set the cook time for 25 minutes. When the cook time ends, use a natural pressure release.

When the valve drops, carefully remove the lid. Transfer the ham hocks to a cutting board to cool. When cool enough to handle, remove the meat from the bones; discard the bones and any fat and gristle. Shred the ham into bite-size pieces.

Stir the ham and salt into the bean mixture. If desired, whisk briskly to break up some of the beans to thicken the soup slightly.

YIELD: Makes 7 cups (1 kg) total

SERVES 6: About 1 cup (175 g) per serving

Nutrition Facts		
SERVING SIZE (175 G)		
AMOUNT PER SERVING		
Calories:	**290**	
		% Daily Value
Total Fat	10g	13%
Saturated Fat	3.5g	18%
Trans Fat	0g	
Cholesterol	45mg	15%
Sodium	470mg	20%
Total Carbohydrate	31g	11%
Dietary Fiber	10g	36%
Total Sugars	4g	
Added Sugars	0g	
Protein	21g	
Vitamin D	0mcg	
Calcium	103mg	8%
Iron	3mg	15%
Potassium	896mg	20%

CUMIN PORK AND CORN STEW WITH AVOCADO

This thick, hearty, rib-sticking soup stew needs no browning! It's the perfect solution when you're tired and hungry and don't want to deal with much prep work!

1¼ pounds (567.5 g) boneless pork chops, trimmed of fat and cut into 1-inch (2.5 cm) pieces

2 onions (8 ounces, or 225 g, total), each cut into 8 wedges

2 cups (330 g) frozen corn

1 (8-ounce, or 225 g) can tomato sauce

2 teaspoons smoked paprika

2 teaspoons ground cumin

2 teaspoons sodium-free beef bouillon granules

2 teaspoons sugar

½ teaspoon garlic powder

1 teaspoon Worcestershire sauce

½ teaspoon salt

½ teaspoon black pepper

½ cup (8 g) chopped fresh cilantro, divided

1 avocado, peeled, pitted, and chopped

1 lime, quartered

In your pressure cooker cooking pot, combine the pork, onions, corn, tomato sauce, paprika, cumin, bouillon granules, sugar, garlic powder, and Worcestershire sauce.

Lock the lid in place and close the seal valve. Press the Manual button to set the cook time for 20 minutes. When the cook time ends, use a natural pressure release.

When the valve drops, carefully remove the lid. Stir in the salt, pepper, and ¼ cup (4 g) of cilantro. Let stand, uncovered, for 10 minutes to thicken slightly and absorb the flavors.

Serve topped with the avocado and lime wedges and remaining ¼ cup (4 g) of cilantro.

YIELD: Makes 6 cups (1.5 kg) total

SERVES 4: 1½ cups (373 g) per serving

Nutrition Facts

SERVING SIZE (373 G)

AMOUNT PER SERVING

Calories: **350**

		% Daily Value
Total Fat	10g	13%
Saturated Fat	2g	10%
Trans Fat	0g	
Cholesterol	80mg	27%
Sodium	680mg	30%
Total Carbohydrate	30g	1%
Dietary Fiber	6g	21%
Total Sugars	8g	
Added Sugars	2g	4%
Protein	38g	
Vitamin D	1mcg	6%
Calcium	36mg	2%
Iron	2mg	10%
Potassium	984mg	20%

PROTEIN AND VEGETABLE COMBINATION DINNERS

There has been a great deal of emphasis on incorporating a variety of green, yellow, and red vegetables into more and more dishes. This helps keep the calorie count low while providing generous serving sizes. Some dishes are served in layers while others are tossed together. Variety, color, and texture all play important nutritional roles, adding interest and character, too. Try using vegetables, instead of the higher-calorie, higher-carb pastas and rice, as a base for a change. You'll be surprised how the new flavor combinations will satisfy, and you may discover some new favorites!

PROTEIN AND VEGETABLE COMBINATION DINNERS

SALMON WITH SPINACH
AND HORSERADISH SOUR CREAM

Pretty, fresh, and f-a-s-t! This can't get any healthier and is one of the easiest recipes in this entire book.

½ cup (115 g) light sour cream

1 tablespoon (15 g) prepared horseradish

¾ teaspoon salt, divided

Nonstick cooking spray, for preparing the cooking pot

1 teaspoon canola oil

2 (9-ounce, or 255 g) package fresh spinach

2 tablespoons (28 g) light butter with canola oil

2 lemons

¾ cup (180 ml) water

4 (6-ounce, or 170 g) frozen salmon fillets

¼ teaspoon black pepper

½ teaspoon dried thyme

In a small bowl, stir together the sour cream, horseradish, and ¼ teaspoon salt. Set aside.

On your pressure cooker, select Sauté/Browning + more to preheat the cooking pot. Once hot, coat the cooking pot with cooking spray. Add the canola oil and tilt the pot to coat the bottom lightly. Add half the spinach. Cook for 2 minutes, or until just beginning to wilt slightly, stirring frequently. Transfer to a dinner or serving plate and set aside.

Coat the cooking pot again with cooking spray. Add the remaining spinach and cook until just wilted. Transfer to the plate with the other spinach. Using the back of a spoon, spread the butter over the spinach and sprinkle with ¼ teaspoon of salt. *Do not stir.* Cover to keep warm.

Slice 1 lemon and place it into the cooking pot. Put a steamer basket into the pot and pour in the water. Place the frozen salmon in the basket. Sprinkle with the remaining ¼ teaspoon of salt, the pepper, and the thyme.

(continued)

Nutrition Facts		
SERVING SIZE (297 G)		
AMOUNT PER SERVING		
Calories:	**260**	
	% Daily Value	
Total Fat	12g	15%
Saturated Fat	4g	20%
Trans Fat	0g	
Cholesterol	75mg	25%
Sodium	690mg	30%
Total Carbohydrate	7g	3%
Dietary Fiber	3g	11%
Total Sugars	0g	
Added Sugars	0g	
Protein	28g	
Vitamin D	0mcg	
Calcium	190mg	15%
Iron	5mg	30%
Potassium	72mg	2%

Lock the lid in place and close the seal valve. Press the Cancel button. Press the Manual button to set the cook time for 4 minutes. When the cook time ends, use a quick pressure release.

When the valve drops, carefully remove the lid. Remove the salmon and place it over the spinach. Squeeze the juice of the remaining lemon over the salmon and top with the sour cream mixture.

YIELD: Makes 4 fillets, 3 cups (540 g) spinach and ½ cup (130 g) sauce total

SERVES 4: About 4 ounces (115 g) cooked salmon, ¾ cup (135 g) spinach, and 2 tablespoons (32.5 g) sauce per serving

GREEK LEMON CHICKEN WITH ASPARAGUS

This is a reverse marinade . . . the assertive ingredients are added at the end, and the chicken soaks up the flavors while resting briefly.

2 teaspoons salt-free grilling blend

1 teaspoon paprika

8 (about 2¼ pounds, or 1 kg, total) bone-in skinless chicken thighs

½ cup (120 ml) dry white wine

½ cup (120 ml) water

2 teaspoons grated lemon zest

2 tablespoons (30 ml) fresh lemon juice

1 tablespoon (15 ml) extra-virgin olive oil

1 garlic clove, minced

2 teaspoons dried dill

½ teaspoon dried oregano

½ teaspoon salt

1 pound (454 g) fresh or frozen cut asparagus

In a small bowl, stir together the seasoning blend and paprika. Sprinkle the spices evenly over the smooth side of the chicken. Pour the white wine and water into the pressure cooker cooking pot. Top with the chicken pieces, overlapping them slightly.

Lock the lid in place and close the seal valve. Press the Manual button to set the cook time for 20 minutes. When the cook time ends, use a natural pressure release for 10 minutes, then a quick pressure release.

When the valve drops, carefully remove the lid. Using a slotted spoon, remove the chicken and place it smooth-side up on a rimmed platter or in a shallow pasta bowl.

In a small bowl, whisk the lemon zest, lemon juice, olive oil, and garlic. Drizzle this all over the chicken. Sprinkle it evenly with the dill, oregano, and salt. Cover with aluminum foil and let rest for 10 minutes to absorb the flavors.

Meanwhile, press the Cancel button. Select Sauté/Browning + more. Bring the liquid in the pot to a boil. Add the asparagus. Return the mixture to a boil and cook for 2 to 3 minutes, or until crisp-tender. Remove with a slotted spoon and arrange around the chicken.

YIELD: Makes 8 chicken thighs and about 4 cups (275 g) asparagus

SERVES 4: 2 chicken thighs and about 1 cup (105 g) asparagus per serving

Nutrition Facts
SERVING SIZE (267 G)

AMOUNT PER SERVING

Calories: **330**

		% Daily Value
Total Fat	14g	18%
Saturated Fat	3.5g	18%
Trans Fat	0g	
Cholesterol	175mg	58%
Sodium	620mg	27%
Total Carbohydrate	13g	5%
Dietary Fiber	4g	14%
Total Sugars	4g	
Added Sugars	0g	
Protein	37g	
Vitamin D	0mcg	
Calcium	44mg	4%
Iron	4mg	20%
Potassium	549mg	10%

CHICKEN CACCIATORE ON BUTTERNUT SQUASH SPIRALS

No need to brown the chicken; it takes on a "browned" appearance when cooking with the smooth side down!

Nonstick cooking spray, for preparing the cooking pot

1½ cups (240 g) chopped onion

1 large green bell pepper, thinly sliced

1 (8-ounce, or 225 g) package sliced mushrooms

1 cup (149 g) grape tomatoes

½ cup (120 ml) dry white wine

1½ tablespoons (23 ml) Worcestershire sauce

1 teaspoon dried oregano

4 bone-in chicken thighs, skin removed (1½ pounds, or 681 g, after removing the skin)

¾ teaspoon salt

2 tablespoons (32 g) tomato paste

1 teaspoon sugar

1 (12-ounce, or 340 g) package frozen butternut squash veggie spirals

On your pressure cooker, select Sauté/Browning + more to preheat the cooking pot. Once hot, coat the pot with cooking spray. Add the onion. Cook for 3 minutes, or until beginning to lightly brown, stirring occasionally. Stir in the green bell pepper, mushrooms, tomatoes, wine, Worcestershire, and oregano. Place the chicken on top, smooth side down, and sprinkle with salt.

Lock the lid in place and close the seal valve. Press the Cancel button. Press the Manual button to set the cook time for 10 minutes. When the cook time ends, use a natural pressure release.

When the valve drops, carefully remove the lid. Using a slotted spoon, transfer the chicken to a rimmed platter or shallow pasta bowl, smooth side up.

Press the Cancel button. Select Sauté/Browning + more. Using a fork, stir in the tomato paste and sugar, breaking up the tomatoes while stirring. Cook, uncovered, for 10 minutes, or until thickened and reduced to 3 cups (720 ml).

Meanwhile, cook the squash in the microwave according to the package directions. Place the squash around the chicken and spoon the vegetable mixture over all.

YIELD: Makes 4 thighs, 3 cups (720 ml) tomato mixture, and 3 cups (630 g) spirals total

SERVES 4: 1 thigh, ¾ cup (180 ml) tomato mixture, and ¾ cup (160 g) spirals per serving

---

Nutrition Facts

SERVING SIZE (394 G)

AMOUNT PER SERVING

Calories: **310**

		% Daily Value
Total Fat	10g	13%
Saturated Fat	2.5g	13%
Trans Fat	0g	
Cholesterol	85mg	28%
Sodium	640mg	28%
Total Carbohydrate	27g	10%
Dietary Fiber	4g	14%
Total Sugars	11g	
Added Sugars	1g	2%
Protein	29g	
Vitamin D	0mcg	
Calcium	77mg	6%
Iron	3mg	15%
Potassium	992mg	20%

PICANTE CHICKEN ON YELLOW SQUASH

Who needs rice?! Lightly browning the squash and onion creates a rich and colorful base for this smoky "enchilada-tasting" dish.

Nonstick cooking spray, for preparing the cooking pot

12 ounces (340 g) yellow crookneck squash, thinly sliced

⅓ cup (53 g) chopped onion

¼ teaspoon black pepper

½ cup (120 ml) water

4 (about 1 pound, or 454 g, total) boneless, skinless, chicken thighs, trimmed of fat

1 cup (240 ml) picante sauce

1 teaspoon smoked paprika

½ teaspoon sugar

On your pressure cooker, select Sauté/Browning + more to preheat the cooking pot. Once hot, coat the pot with cooking spray. Add the squash, onion, and pepper. Cook for 5 minutes, or until just crisp-tender and beginning to lightly brown, stirring frequently. Transfer the mixture to a plate and cover with aluminum foil to keep warm.

Add the water to the cooking pot, scraping up any browned bits from the bottom of the pot. Add the chicken, picante sauce, and paprika.

Lock the lid in place and close the seal valve. Press the Cancel button. Press the Manual button to set the cook time for 8 minutes. When the cook time ends, use a quick pressure release.

When the valve drops, carefully remove the lid. Using a slotted spoon, remove the chicken and place it on the squash mixture. Re-cover and set aside.

Press the Cancel button. Select Sauté/Browning + more. Stir the sugar into the sauce and bring it to a boil. Boil for 5 minutes, or until reduced to 1 cup (240 ml). Spoon the sauce over the chicken and squash.

YIELD: Makes 3 cups (408 g) squash, 12 ounces (340 g) cooked chicken, and 1 cup (240 ml) sauce

SERVES 4: ¾ cup (102 g) squash, 3 ounces (85 g) cooked chicken, and ¼ cup (60 ml) sauce per serving

Nutrition Facts

SERVING SIZE (247 G)

AMOUNT PER SERVING

Calories: **200**

		% Daily Value
Total Fat	8g	10%
Saturated Fat	2.5g	13%
Trans Fat	0g	
Cholesterol	75mg	2%
Sodium	570mg	25%
Total Carbohydrate	9g	3%
Dietary Fiber	2g	7%
Total Sugars	6g	
Added Sugars	1g	2%
Protein	22g	
Vitamin D	0mcg	
Calcium	30mg	2%
Iron	2mg	10%
Potassium	362mg	8%

CHEESY BEEF AND CORN-STUFFED POBLANOS

Scrumptious to look at and even *more* scrumptious to eat. These knife-and-fork stuffed peppers go way beyond the ordinary with their double chiles, corn, and smoky cumin flavors— *and* they're smothered in cheese!

8 ounces (225 g) lean ground beef

1 (4.5-ounce, or 130 g) can mild chopped green chiles

1 cup (165 g) frozen corn

1 teaspoon smoked paprika

1 teaspoon ground cumin

¼ teaspoon salt

4 large poblano peppers, tops removed, seeded, leaving the pepper whole

1 cup (240 ml) water

4 ounces (115 g) shredded reduced-fat Mexican cheese blend

½ cup (90 g) chopped tomatoes

In a medium bowl, mix together the ground beef, green chiles, corn, paprika, cumin, and salt. Spoon equal amounts of the beef mixture into each pepper.

Put a trivet into your pressure cooker cooking pot and pour in the water. Arrange the peppers on the trivet, propping them up so they lean against the pot's wall.

Lock the lid in place and close the seal valve. Press the Manual button to set the cook time for 10 minutes. When the cook time ends, use a natural pressure release for 10 minutes, then a quick pressure release.

When the valve drops, carefully remove the lid. Using tongs or a fork and spoon, gently remove the peppers and place them on plates on their sides. Sprinkle evenly with the cheese and the tomatoes. Let stand, uncovered, for 5 minutes to absorb the flavors and for the cheese to melt.

YIELD: Makes 4 stuffed peppers

SERVES 4: 1 pepper per serving

Nutrition Facts

SERVING SIZE (261 G)

AMOUNT PER SERVING

Calories: **240**

		% Daily Value
Total Fat	10g	13%
Saturated Fat	5g	25%
Trans Fat	0g	
Cholesterol	55mg	18%
Sodium	520mg	23%
Total Carbohydrate	18g	7%
Dietary Fiber	3g	11%
Total Sugars	6g	
Added Sugars	0g	
Protein	22g	
Vitamin D	0mcg	
Calcium	360mg	30%
Iron	3mg	15%
Potassium	487mg	10%

FLANK STRIPS WITH SWEET BALSAMIC GLAZE ON ARUGULA

By thinly slicing the beef before you cook it, you help the rich sweet sauce to penetrate throughout every slice. Serve it over arugula to highlight the deep flavors!

1¼ pounds (568 g) flank steak, cut across the grain into thin strips

1 cup (240 ml) light beer (such as Miller Lite)

8 garlic cloves, peeled

2 tablespoons (30 ml) balsamic vinegar

2 tablespoons (30 ml) light soy sauce

1 tablespoon (15 ml) Worcestershire sauce

1 tablespoon (12.5 g) sugar

¼ teaspoon salt

Pinch cayenne pepper

4 cups (80 g) arugula

In your pressure cooker cooking pot, combine the beef, beer, and garlic.

Lock the lid in place and close the seal valve. Press the Manual button to set the cook time for 10 minutes. When the cook time ends, use a natural pressure release.

When the valve drops, carefully remove the lid. Remove the beef and garlic and set aside. Reserve ¼ cup (60 ml) of the cooking liquid and discard the rest.

Press the Cancel button. Select Sauté/Browning + more. Return the reserved ¼ cup (60 ml) of cooking liquid to the pot and add the vinegar, soy sauce, Worcestershire sauce, sugar, salt, and cayenne. Bring the mixture to a boil. Boil for 3 minutes.

Return the beef and garlic to the pot. Cook for 2 minutes, or until the meat is glazed and the liquid has evaporated, stirring frequently. Serve the beef over the arugula.

YIELD: Makes 12 ounces (340 g) cooked beef and 4 cups (80 g) arugula

SERVES 4: 3 ounces (85 g) cooked beef and 1 cup (20 g) arugula per serving

Nutrition Facts

SERVING SIZE (105 G)

AMOUNT PER SERVING

Calories: **240**

		% Daily Value
Total Fat	8g	10%
Saturated Fat	3g	15%
Trans Fat	0g	
Cholesterol	90mg	30%
Sodium	570mg	25%
Total Carbohydrate	8g	3%
Dietary Fiber	0g	
Total Sugars	5g	
Added Sugars	3g	6%
Protein	32g	
Vitamin D	0mcg	
Calcium	77mg	6%
Iron	3mg	15%
Potassium	580mg	10%

BARBECUE MEATLOAF AND FRESH CORN ON THE COB

No heating the oven, no boiling big pots of water . . . it's all cooked in one pot and keeps the kitchen cool!

1 cup plus 1½ tablespoons (263 ml) water

⅓ cup (85 g) barbecue sauce

12 ounces (340 g) extra-lean ground beef

2 jalapeño peppers, seeded and finely chopped

½ cup (80 g) finely chopped onion

⅔ cup (54 g) quick-cooking oats

2 large egg whites

1 teaspoon dried oregano

¼ teaspoon salt, divided

Nonstick cooking spray, for preparing the foil sheets

4 fresh ears corn, shucked

4 teaspoons (19 g) light butter with canola oil

⅛ teaspoon black pepper

Put a trivet into your pressure cooker cooking pot and pour in 1 cup (240 ml) of water.

In a small bowl, stir together the barbecue sauce and remaining 1½ tablespoons (23 ml) of water.

In a medium bowl, mix together the ground beef, jalapeños, onion, oats, egg whites, oregano, ⅛ teaspoon of salt, and 3 tablespoons (48 g) of the barbecue sauce mixture. Shape into a 4-by-6-by-2-inch (10 by 15 by 5 cm) loaf.

Tear off three (18-inch, or 45 cm) sheets of aluminum foil and fold each sheet in half lengthwise. Coat the strips with cooking spray. Crisscross the strips in a spokelike fashion to act as a sling. Place the loaf in the center of the spokes. Lift the ends of the foil strips to transfer the loaf to the trivet. Fold down the foil strips so they won't interfere with closing the lid.

Lock the lid in place and close the seal valve. Press the Manual button to set the cook time for 35 minutes. When the cook time ends, use a quick pressure release.

Nutrition Facts

SERVING SIZE (261 G)

AMOUNT PER SERVING

Calories: **350**

		% Daily Value
Total Fat	11g	14%
Saturated Fat	3.5g	18%
Trans Fat	0g	
Cholesterol	55mg	18%
Sodium	490mg	21%
Total Carbohydrate	40g	15%
Dietary Fiber	4g	14%
Total Sugars	14g	
Added Sugars	0g	
Protein	26g	
Vitamin D	0mcg	
Calcium	31mg	2%
Iron	3mg	15%
Potassium	432mg	10%

When the valve drops, carefully remove the lid. Using the ends of the foil, carefully remove the meatloaf and place it on a cutting board. Spoon the remaining barbecue sauce evenly over the meatloaf and let stand for 10 minutes before slicing.

Meanwhile, place the corn on the trivet.

Lock the lid in place and close the seal valve. Press the Cancel button. Press the Manual button to set the cook time for 2 minutes. When the cook time ends, use a quick pressure release.

Top each ear of corn with 1 teaspoon of butter and sprinkle with the remaining ⅛ teaspoon of salt and the pepper. Serve alongside the meatloaf.

YIELD: Makes 1 meatloaf and 4 ears corn

SERVES 4: ¼ meatloaf and 1 ear corn per serving

ITALIAN MEATBALLS AND SIMPLE SAUCE ON ZUCCHINI NOODLES

When buying prepared spaghetti sauce, look for those that contain the lowest sodium. You have more control over your sodium intake that way . . . even if you need to add a bit more salt to the final dish.

12 ounces (340 g) 93% lean ground turkey

1 (3.5-ounce, or 100 g) Italian turkey sausage link, casing removed

⅔ cup (33 g) panko bread crumbs

½ cup (30 g) finely chopped fresh parsley

2 large eggs, beaten

2 teaspoons dried basil

1 teaspoon dried rosemary

½ teaspoon dried fennel

¼ teaspoon red pepper flakes

Nonstick cooking spray, for preparing the cooking pot

2 cups (500 g) prepared lower-sodium spaghetti sauce (such as Prego Heart Smart)

½ cup (120 ml) red wine

2 teaspoons honey

1 (12-ounce, or 340 g) package frozen zucchini spirals

4 teaspoons (8 g) grated Parmesan cheese

In a medium bowl, mix together the ground turkey, sausage, bread crumbs, parsley, beaten eggs, basil, rosemary, fennel, and red pepper flakes. Shape the mixture into about 32 small (1-inch, or 2.5 cm) balls.

On your pressure cooker, select Sauté/Browning + more to preheat the cooking pot. Once hot, coat the pot with cooking spray. Add the meatballs to the pot in a single layer (it will be snug). Cook for 3 minutes, *without turning*.

In the medium bowl, stir together the spaghetti sauce and red wine. Pour the sauce evenly over the meatballs. *Do not stir.*

Lock the lid in place and close the seal valve. Press the Cancel button. Press the Manual button to set the cook time for 4 minutes. When the cook time ends, use a quick pressure release.

When the valve drops, carefully remove the lid. Drizzle the honey over all and gently toss to combine.

Meanwhile, cook the zucchini spirals according to the package directions. Serve the meatballs and sauce over the zucchini and sprinkle with the Parmesan.

Nutrition Facts

SERVING SIZE (402 G)

AMOUNT PER SERVING

Calories: 330

		% Daily Value
Total Fat	9g	12%
Saturated Fat	1.5g	8%
Trans Fat	0g	
Cholesterol	145mg	48%
Sodium	680mg	30%
Total Carbohydrate	27g	10%
Dietary Fiber	1g	4%
Total Sugars	15g	
Added Sugars	3g	6%
Protein	34g	
Vitamin D	1mcg	6%
Calcium	123mg	10%
Iron	4mg	20%
Potassium	717mg	15%

YIELD: Makes 32 meatballs, 1¾ cups (420 ml) sauce, and about 3 cups (340 g) zucchini

SERVES 4: 8 meatballs, about ¾ cup (180 ml) sauce, and about ¾ cup (85 g) zucchini per serving

BEEF AND SHELLS WITH TOMATOES

A kid favorite for sure! Not a fan of green bell peppers? Substitute red peppers and finely chop them! With all the red from the tomatoes and tomato sauce, you'll be able to sneak them in!

Nonstick cooking spray, for preparing the cooking pot

1 pound (454 g) lean ground beef

1½ cups (225 g) chopped green bell pepper

1 cup (160 g) chopped onion

4 ounces (115 g) whole-grain or white-fiber pasta shells

1 (14.5-ounce, or 410 g) can diced tomatoes with basil, oregano, and garlic

1 (8-ounce, or 240 ml) can tomato sauce

1 cup (240 ml) water

2 teaspoons Worcestershire sauce

1 tablespoon (15 g) ketchup

⅛ teaspoon salt

On your pressure cooker, select Sauté/Browning + more to preheat the cooking pot. Once hot, coat the pot with cooking spray. Add the ground beef. Cook for 3 minutes, or until browned, stirring occasionally. Add the green bell pepper, onion, pasta, tomatoes, tomato sauce, water, and Worcestershire sauce.

Lock the lid in place and close the seal valve. Press the Cancel button. Press the Manual button to set the cook time for 4 minutes. When the cook time ends, use a quick pressure release.

When the valve drops, carefully remove the lid. Stir in the ketchup and salt. Let stand, uncovered, for 10 minutes to absorb the liquid.

YIELD: Makes 6 cups (1.5 kg) total

SERVES 4: 1½ cups (386 g) per serving

Nutrition Facts

SERVING SIZE (386 G)

AMOUNT PER SERVING

Calories: **340**

		% Daily Value
Total Fat	9g	12%
Saturated Fat	4g	20%
Trans Fat	0g	
Cholesterol	70mg	23%
Sodium	710mg	31%
Total Carbohydrate	38g	14%
Dietary Fiber	4g	14%
Total Sugars	9g	
Added Sugars	0g	
Protein	29g	
Vitamin D	0mcg	
Calcium	150mg	10%
Iron	3mg	15%
Potassium	342mg	8%

BEEF AND EGGPLANT

Get 100 percent of your vitamin C with this Middle Eastern dish of pecans, beef, eggplant, sweet peppers, raisins, and tomatoes, cooked with heady sweet spices and served topped with yogurt.

2 ounces (55 g) chopped pecans or slivered almonds

Nonstick cooking spray, for preparing the cooking pot

12 ounces (340 g) lean ground beef

8 ounces (225 g) chopped eggplant

1 cup (160 g) chopped onion

1 large red bell pepper, coarsely chopped

⅓ cup (50 g) raisins

1 (10.75-ounce, or 305 g) can diced tomatoes with green chiles

1 teaspoon ground cinnamon

¼ teaspoon ground nutmeg

1½ teaspoons sugar

¼ teaspoon salt

½ cup (115 g) 2% plain Greek yogurt

On your pressure cooker, select Sauté/Browning + more to preheat the cooking pot. Once hot, add the nuts to the pot. Cook for 4 minutes, stirring occasionally. Remove from the pot and set aside. Coat the pot with cooking spray. Add the ground beef. Cook for 4 minutes, stirring frequently. Add the eggplant, onion, red bell pepper, raisins, tomatoes and chiles, cinnamon, and nutmeg.

Lock the lid in place and close the seal valve. Press the Cancel button. Press the Manual button to set the cook time for 12 minutes. When the cook time ends, use a quick pressure release.

When the valve drops, carefully remove the lid. Press the Cancel button. Select Sauté/Browning + more. Stir in the sugar, salt, and pecans. Bring to a boil and cook for 6 minutes, or until thickened slightly. Let stand, uncovered, for 5 minutes to absorb the flavors. Serve topped with yogurt.

YIELD: Makes about 5 cups (1.3 kg) total

SERVES 4: About 1¼ cups (328 g) per serving

Nutrition Facts

SERVING SIZE (328 G)

AMOUNT PER SERVING

Calories: **320**

		% Daily Value
Total Fat	16g	21%
Saturated Fat	4g	20%
Trans Fat	0g	
Cholesterol	55mg	18%
Sodium	530mg	23%
Total Carbohydrate	26g	9%
Dietary Fiber	5g	18%
Total Sugars	19g	
Added Sugars	2g	4%
Protein	21g	
Vitamin D	0mcg	
Calcium	46mg	4%
Iron	1mg	6%
Potassium	436mg	10%

ITALIAN SAUSAGE–STUFFED PEPPERS

When purchasing bell peppers, choose the wider, fatter variety rather than the narrower ones. They're easier to fill and keep their balance while cooking.

12 ounces (340 g) ground Italian turkey sausage

4 large bell peppers, any color; tops cut off, chopped, and reserved; seeded

¼ cup (20 g) oats, any variety

¾ cup (184 g) no-salt-added tomato sauce, divided

1 large egg

⅛ teaspoon red pepper flakes

1 cup (240 ml) water

1 ounce (28 g) shredded part-skim mozzarella cheese

2 tablespoons (12.5 g) grated Parmesan cheese

In a medium bowl, mix together the turkey sausage, chopped pepper tops, oats, ¼ cup (61 g) of tomato sauce, the egg, and the red pepper flakes. Divide the turkey mixture into 4 portions, and stuff each pepper with 1 portion.

Put a trivet into the pressure cooker cooking pot and pour in the water. Arrange the stuffed peppers on the trivet. Top each pepper with 2 tablespoons of the remaining tomato sauce.

Lock the lid in place and close the seal valve. Press the Manual button to set the cook time for 15 minutes. When the cook time ends, use a natural pressure release.

When the valve drops, carefully remove the lid. Top the peppers with equal amounts of the mozzarella and Parmesan cheeses.

YIELD: Makes 4 stuffed peppers

SERVES 4: 1 stuffed pepper per serving

Nutrition Facts
SERVING SIZE (325 G)

AMOUNT PER SERVING
Calories: 280

		% Daily Value
Total Fat	14g	18%
Saturated Fat	2g	10%
Trans Fat	0g	
Cholesterol	105mg	35%
Sodium	700mg	30%
Total Carbohydrate	17g	6%
Dietary Fiber	4g	14%
Total Sugars	8g	
Added Sugars	0g	
Protein	22g	
Vitamin D	0mcg	
Calcium	119mg	10%
Iron	3mg	15%
Potassium	343mg	8%

SAUSAGE ON GREENS WITH PEPPER OIL

No need to boil away all the nutrients. The pressure cooker seals in all the natural flavors and nutrients of the collards and the chicken sausage. The hot pepper oil adds just the right amount of seasoning.

Nonstick cooking spray, for preparing the cooking pot

4 (3-ounce, or 85 g) chicken and apple sausage links (such as Al Fresco)

1 (16-oz, or 454 g) package chopped fresh collard greens

2 quarts (1.9 L) water

1½ teaspoons sugar

1 teaspoon dried thyme

½ teaspoon garlic powder

¼ teaspoon salt

2 tablespoons (30 ml) extra-virgin olive oil

2 teaspoons hot sauce (such as Frank's)

On your pressure cooker, select Sauté/Browning + more to preheat the cooking pot. Once hot, coat the pot with cooking spray. Add the sausage. Cook for 8 minutes, turning occasionally. Remove and set aside.

Place the collards into the pot. Pour in the water. Sprinkle with the sugar, thyme, and garlic powder. Top with the sausage.

Lock the lid in place and close the seal valve. Press the Cancel button. Press the Manual to set the cook time for 20 minutes. When the cook time ends, use a quick pressure release.

When the valve drops, carefully remove the lid (the sausage may have split slightly while cooking).

Drain the collards, reserving ⅓ cup (80 ml) of cooking liquid. Place the collards in a shallow pan or pasta bowl. Add the salt to the reserved cooking liquid and pour it over the collards. Top with the sausage, split side down.

In a small bowl, whisk the olive oil and hot sauce. Drizzle evenly over all.

YIELD: Makes 4 sausages, about 4 cups (520 g) greens, and about 2½ tablespoons (38 ml) pepper oil total

SERVES 4: 1 sausage, 1 cup (130 g) greens, and 2 teaspoons pepper oil per serving

Nutrition Facts

SERVING SIZE (209 G)

AMOUNT PER SERVING

Calories: **260**

		% Daily Value
Total Fat	15g	19%
Saturated Fat	3g	15%
Trans Fat	0g	
Cholesterol	60mg	20%
Sodium	870mg	38%
Total Carbohydrate	16g	6%
Dietary Fiber	5g	18%
Total Sugars	10g	
Added Sugars	0g	
Protein	17g	
Vitamin D	0mcg	
Calcium	264mg	20%
Iron	2mg	10%
Potassium	246mg	6%

TENDER PORK CHOPS IN RICH ONION SAUCE

The secret seasoning in this dish is not a particular herb or spice . . . it's browning the onions!

Nonstick cooking spray, for preparing the cooking pot

1 teaspoon canola oil

2 cups (320 g) thinly sliced onions

1 cup (240 ml) water

1 teaspoon balsamic vinegar

4 (8-ounce, or 225 g) bone-in pork loin chops, about 1-inch (2.5 cm) thick, trimmed of fat

2 teaspoons sodium-free beef bouillon granulates

¾ teaspoon black pepper

½ teaspoon paprika

½ teaspoon garlic powder

½ teaspoon salt, divided

¼ teaspoon sugar

On your pressure cooker, select Sauté/Browning + more to preheat the cooking pot. Once hot, coat the pot with cooking spray. Add the canola oil and tilt the pot to coat the bottom lightly. Add the onions. Cook for 10 minutes, stirring occasionally. Stir in the water and vinegar. Place the pork chops on top. Sprinkle with the bouillon granules, pepper, paprika, garlic powder, and ¼ teaspoon of salt.

Lock the lid in place and close the seal valve. Press the Cancel button. Press the Manual button to set the cook time for 18 minutes. When the cook time ends, use a natural pressure release for 10 minutes, then a quick pressure release.

When the valve drops, carefully remove the lid. Add the remaining ¼ teaspoon of salt and the sugar to the mixture in the pot. Stir, making sure the pork chops are covered with the onion mixture.

Press the Cancel button. Select Sauté/Browning + more. Bring the mixture to a boil. Cook for 10 minutes, or until the onion mixture is slightly thickened and reduced to 1 cup (100 g).

YIELD: Makes 4 pork chops and 1 cup (100 g) onion mixture

SERVES 4: About 5 ounces (140 g) cooked pork and ¼ cup (25 g) onion mixture per serving

Nutrition Facts

SERVING SIZE (165 G)

AMOUNT PER SERVING

Calories: 240

		% Daily Value
Total Fat	7g	9%
Saturated Fat	2g	10%
Trans Fat	0g	
Cholesterol	110mg	37%
Sodium	380mg	17%
Total Carbohydrate	8g	3%
Dietary Fiber	1g	4%
Total Sugars	4g	
Added Sugars	0g	
Protein	35g	
Vitamin D	1mcg	6%
Calcium	47mg	4%
Iron	1mg	6%
Potassium	683mg	15%

SWEETS AND DESSERTS

Just because they're low calorie, desserts don't have to taste "light" . . . not at all! Nor do they have to take a lot of time to make. And, with these recipes, there is absolutely no need to turn on a big oven to bake your desserts. The pressure cooker does the work and keeps the heat out of the kitchen!

SWEETS
AND DESSERTS

APPLE HALVES WITH VANILLA "CREAM" SAUCE

This dish actually has two sauces: one, a simple sweet, creamy sauce made in the pot before the apples are cooked, and the other, a reduction of pan juices made after the apples are cooked. The apples are drizzled with one and surrounded by the other!

1 cup (240 ml) 2% milk

1 tablespoon (8 g) cornstarch

2 tablespoons (25 g) sugar

1 teaspoon vanilla extract

1 cup (240 ml) water

2 large (about 1 pound, or 454 g, total) red apples (such as Envy or Honeycrisp), halved and cored

¼ teaspoon ground cinnamon

1 tablespoon (14 g) light butter with canola oil

On your pressure cooker, select Sauté/Browning + more to preheat the cooking pot. In a small bowl, whisk the milk and cornstarch until the cornstarch dissolves. Once the pot is hot, pour the milk mixture into the pot and add the sugar. Bring to a boil. Boil for 1 minute, or until thickened. Return the milk mixture to the small bowl, whisk in the vanilla, and refrigerate until serving.

Put a trivet into the pressure cooker cooking pot and pour in the water. Place the apples, flat side up, on the trivet. Sprinkle evenly with the cinnamon.

Lock the lid in place and close the seal valve. Press the Cancel button. Press the Manual button to set the cook time for 10 minutes. When the cook time ends, use a quick pressure release.

When the valve drops, carefully remove the lid. Press the Cancel button. Select Sauté/Browning + more. Divide the apples among 4 dessert bowls. Top with equal amounts of butter. Remove the trivet from the pot.

Bring the liquid in the pot to a boil. Boil for 7 minutes, or until reduced to 2 tablespoons (30 ml). Spoon the reduced liquid over the apples and spoon the "cream" sauce around the apples.

YIELD: Makes 4 apple halves, 2 tablespoons (30 ml) syrup, and 1 cup (240 ml) cream sauce

SERVES 4: 1 apple half, 1½ teaspoons syrup, and ¼ cup (60 ml) cream sauce per serving

Nutrition Facts

SERVING SIZE (159 G)

AMOUNT PER SERVING

Calories: **120**

		% Daily Value
Total Fat	2.5g	3%
Saturated Fat	1.5g	8%
Trans Fat	0g	
Cholesterol	5mg	2%
Sodium	50mg	2%
Total Carbohydrate	23g	8%
Dietary Fiber	2g	7%
Total Sugars	18g	
Added Sugars	6g	12%
Protein	2g	
Vitamin D	1mcg	6%
Calcium	79mg	6%
Iron	0mg	0%
Potassium	178mg	4%

HOT CURRIED FRUIT

Every one of these ingredients can be kept on hand, so all you have to do is throw them in the pot whenever you want! This is delicious served as a warm treat or at room temp. Serve the next day over 2 percent fat plain Greek yogurt for a refreshing breakfast dish, too.

1 cup (140 g) frozen pineapple chunks

1 cup (140 g) frozen mango chunks

1 cup (140 g) frozen sliced peaches

1 tablespoon (9 g) raisins or dried cranberries, halved

1 cup plus 1 tablespoon (255 ml) water, divided

1 tablespoon (8 g) cornstarch

1½ tablespoons (23 g) packed dark brown sugar

1½ teaspoons curry powder

1 teaspoon vanilla extract

2 tablespoons (28 g) light butter with canola oil

In your pressure cooker cooking pot, combine the pineapple, mango, peaches, raisins, and 1 cup (240 ml) of water.

Lock the lid in place and close the seal valve. Press the Manual button to set the cook time for 8 minutes. When the cook time ends, use a quick pressure release.

When the valve drops, carefully remove the lid. Press the Cancel button. Select Sauté/Browning + more. In a small bowl, stir together the remaining 1 tablespoon (15 ml) of water and the cornstarch until the cornstarch dissolves. Stir this slurry into the fruit mixture along with the brown sugar and curry powder. Bring to a boil. Cook for 1 minute, stirring constantly. Turn off the pressure cooker. Stir in the vanilla and butter. Let stand, uncovered, for 5 minutes to absorb the flavors. Serve hot or cold.

YIELD: Makes 2 cups (564 g) total

SERVES 4: ½ cup (141 g) per serving

Nutrition Facts
SERVING SIZE (141 G)

AMOUNT PER SERVING
Calories: **110**

		% Daily Value
Total Fat	1.5g	2%
Saturated Fat	0.5g	3%
Trans Fat	0g	
Cholesterol	0mg	
Sodium	60mg	3%
Total Carbohydrate	25g	9%
Dietary Fiber	2g	7%
Total Sugars	17g	
Added Sugars	5g	10%
Protein	1g	
Vitamin D	0mcg	
Calcium	7mg	0%
Iron	0mg	
Potassium	48mg	2%

APPLE-CRANBERRY OAT CRUMBLE

Get the flavors and texture of "home baked" without having to heat up the oven or kitchen or wait before you can actually eat it. "Toasting" the topping in the pressure cooker cooking pot first, then topping the cooked apple mixture with it, is all that's needed.

FOR TOPPING:

½ cup quick-cooking (40 g) or old-fashioned (78 g) rolled oats

1 ounce (28 g) chopped pecans

¼ teaspoon ground cinnamon

⅛ teaspoon ground nutmeg

1 tablespoon (15 g) packed dark brown sugar

¼ teaspoon salt

FOR BASE:

1 cup plus 1 tablespoon (255 ml) water, divided

3 cups (375 g) chopped apples

2 tablespoons (15 g) dried cranberries, halved

1½ teaspoons cornstarch

2 tablespoons (30 g) packed dark brown sugar

1 tablespoon (14 g) light butter with canola oil

1 teaspoon vanilla extract

TO MAKE THE TOPPING: On your pressure cooker, select Sauté/Browning + more to preheat the cooking pot. Once hot, add the oats, pecans, cinnamon, and nutmeg to the pot. Cook for 5 minutes, stirring frequently. Stir in the brown sugar and salt. Transfer the topping to a plate and set aside.

TO MAKE THE BASE: In the pressure cooker cooking pot, combine 1 cup (240 ml) of water, the apples, and the dried cranberries.

Lock the lid in place and close the seal valve. Press the Cancel button. Press the Manual button to set the cook time for 4 minutes. When the cook time ends, use a quick pressure release.

When the valve drops, carefully remove the lid. Press the Cancel button. Select Sauté/Browning + more. In a small bowl, whisk the remaining 1 tablespoon (15 ml) of water and the cornstarch until the cornstarch dissolves. Stir this slurry into the fruit mixture along with the brown sugar. Bring to a boil. Boil for 1 minute, stirring constantly. Turn off the pressure cooker. Stir in the butter and vanilla. Transfer the fruit mixture to a shallow bowl or casserole dish.

Top with the oat mixture and let stand, uncovered, for 15 minutes to absorb the flavors.

YIELD: Makes 3 cups (772 g) total

SERVES 4: ¾ cup (193 g) per serving

Nutrition Facts		
SERVING SIZE (128 G)		
AMOUNT PER SERVING		
Calories:	**200**	
		% Daily Value
Total Fat	7g	9%
Saturated Fat	1g	5%
Trans Fat	0g	
Cholesterol	0mg	
Sodium	60mg	3%
Total Carbohydrate	33g	12%
Dietary Fiber	5g	18%
Total Sugars	20g	
Added Sugars	6g	12%
Protein	2g	
Vitamin D	0mcg	
Calcium	17mg	2%
Iron	1mg	6%
Potassium	175mg	4%

KIWI CITRUS TEA CAKE

This cake-based fruited dessert is so delicate because of the pear and egg whites added to the batter. It's served topped with a light orange citrus sauce and fresh kiwi slices.

FOR CAKE:

1 (9-ounce, or 255 g) single-layer yellow cake mix

1½ cups (360 ml) water, divided

2 ounces (55 g) puréed pears (such as a baby food variety)

2 large egg whites

1 teaspoon grated orange zest

Nonstick cooking spray, for preparing the springform pan

FOR SAUCE:

½ cup (120 ml) fresh orange juice

1 tablespoon (12.5 g) sugar

2 teaspoons cornstarch

½ teaspoon grated orange zest

2 teaspoons light butter with canola oil

2 kiwi, peeled and chopped

TO MAKE THE CAKE: In a medium bowl, combine the cake mix, ½ cup (120 ml) of water, and the puréed pears, egg whites, and orange zest. Whisk for 1 minute, or until well blended.

Put a trivet into the pressure cooker cooking pot and pour in the remaining 1 cup (240 ml) of water. Coat an 8-inch (20 cm) springform pan with cooking spray. Pour the batter into the prepared pan. Wrap the entire pan with aluminum foil. Make a foil sling by folding a 20-inch (50 cm)–long piece of foil in half lengthwise. Place the pan in the center of the sling and lower the pan into the pot. Fold down the excess foil to allow the lid to close properly (the pan will fit snugly).

Lock the lid in place and close the seal valve. Press the Manual button to set the cook time for 15 minutes. When the cook time ends, use a quick release.

When the valve drops, carefully remove the lid. Using the foil sling, transfer the pan to a wire rack. Remove all the foil. Cool completely (the texture will change while cooling).

Nutrition Facts		
SERVING SIZE (84 G)		
AMOUNT PER SERVING		
Calories:	**160**	
	% Daily Value	
Total Fat	1.5g	2%
Saturated Fat	0.5g	3%
Trans Fat	0g	
Cholesterol	0mg	
Sodium	250mg	11%
Total Carbohydrate	34g	12%
Dietary Fiber	1g	4%
Total Sugars	18g	
Added Sugars	2g	4%
Protein	2g	
Vitamin D	0mcg	
Calcium	77mg	6%
Iron	1mg	6%
Potassium	121mg	2%

TO MAKE THE SAUCE: Meanwhile, remove the trivet and discard the water in the pot. Press the Cancel button. Select Sauté/Browning + more. In a small bowl, whisk the orange juice, sugar, and cornstarch until smooth.

Once the pot is hot, add the juice mixture. Bring to a boil. Boil for 1 minute, stirring constantly, or until thickened. Return to the bowl and stir in the orange zest and butter. Set aside to cool and thicken.

To serve, carefully remove the sides of the pan. Cut the cake into wedges. Top with equal amounts of the sauce and kiwi.

YIELD: Makes one 8-inch (20 cm) tea cake, ½ cup (120 ml) sauce, and 2 kiwi

SERVES 8: ⅛ tea cake, 1 tablespoon (15 ml) sauce, and ¼ kiwi per serving

MINI FLANS WITH ESPRESSO

Wrapping each custard dish entirely with aluminum foil prevents any water or steam from getting into the egg mixture. Use tongs or a clean cloth to remove each dish easily and safely when finished cooking.

⅔ cup (160 ml) fat-free evaporated milk

½ cup (120 ml) 2% milk

⅓ cup (107 g) pure maple syrup

2 large eggs

1 teaspoon vanilla extract

⅛ teaspoon ground nutmeg

⅛ teaspoon salt

Nonstick cooking spray, for preparing the ramekins

1 cup (240 ml) water

FOR ESPRESSO:

2 tablespoons (30 ml) water

1 teaspoon sugar

¼ teaspoon instant coffee granules

¼ teaspoon vanilla extract

In a medium bowl, whisk the evaporated milk, 2% milk, maple syrup, eggs, vanilla, nutmeg, and salt.

Coat four 6-ounce (180 ml) ramekins or custard cups with cooking spray. Place an equal amount of the egg mixture in each ramekin. Wrap each entirely with aluminum foil.

Put a trivet into the pressure cooker cooking pot and pour in the water. Place 3 ramekins on the trivet and top with the remaining ramekin.

Lock the lid in place and close the seal valve. Press the Manual button to set the cook time for 8 minutes. When the cook time ends, use a natural pressure release for 10 minutes, then a quick release.

When the valve drops, carefully remove the lid. Transfer the ramekins to a cooling rack. Carefully remove the foil. Cool completely. Cover and refrigerate until serving.

TO MAKE THE ESPRESSO: In a cup or small bowl, stir together the espresso ingredients until the sugar dissolves.

When serving, invert the ramekins onto 4 dessert plates and spoon equal amounts of espresso over each.

YIELD: Makes 4 flans and 2 tablespoons (30 ml) espresso total

SERVES 4: 1 flan and 1½ teaspoons espresso per serving

Nutrition Facts

SERVING SIZE (127 G)

AMOUNT PER SERVING

Calories: **160**

		% Daily Value
Total Fat	3g	4%
Saturated Fat	1g	5%
Trans Fat	0g	
Cholesterol	95mg	32%
Sodium	170mg	7%
Total Carbohydrate	26g	9%
Dietary Fiber	0g	
Total Sugars	24g	
Added Sugars	17g	34%
Protein	7g	
Vitamin D	2mcg	10%
Calcium	201mg	15%
Iron	1mg	6%
Potassium	277mg	6%

WHITE WINE–POACHED PEARS

Five ingredients. That's all it takes to make these syrupy tender pears. The technique is in the cooling time. The liquid thickens and turns into a rich syrup as it cools.

1 cup (240 ml) white wine

2 (about 1 pound, or 454 g, total) firm pears, peeled, halved, and cored

⅛ teaspoon ground cinnamon

2 tablespoons (25 g) sugar

1 teaspoon light butter with canola oil

Put a steamer basket into your pressure cooker cooking pot and pour in the wine. Place the pears, flat side down, in the basket. Sprinkle evenly with the cinnamon.

Lock the lid in place and close the seal valve. Press the Manual button to set the cook time for 7 minutes. When the cook time ends, use a quick pressure release (the pears will be crisp-tender, but will continue to soften while standing).

When the valve drops, carefully remove the lid. Press the Cancel button. Select Sauté/Browning + more. Place the pears in a shallow dish and remove the steamer basket. Add the sugar to the liquid in the pot. Bring to a boil. Cook for 3 minutes, or until reduced to ¼ cup (60 ml).

Turn off the pressure cooker. Stir in the butter until melted and pour the liquid over the pears. Turn the pears several times to coat. Let stand, uncovered, for 30 minutes, turning occasionally.

YIELD: Makes 4 pear halves and ¼ cup (60 ml) sauce total

SERVES 4: ½ pear plus 1 tablespoon (15 ml) sauce per serving

Nutrition Facts

SERVING SIZE (136 G)

AMOUNT PER SERVING

Calories: **140**

		% Daily Value
Total Fat	4.5g	6%
Saturated Fat	0.5g	3%
Trans Fat	0g	
Cholesterol	0mg	
Sodium	15mg	1%
Total Carbohydrate	25g	9%
Dietary Fiber	4g	14%
Total Sugars	18g	
Added Sugars	6g	12%
Protein	2g	
Vitamin D	0mcg	
Calcium	30mg	2%
Iron	0mg	
Potassium	180mg	4%

BANANA CHOCOLATE CHIP PEANUT BUTTER WEDGES

These thin cakelike wedges are topped with a layer of nut butter and served smothered with chopped bananas and cinnamon sugar. You'll feel like a kid again with every bite!

Nonstick cooking spray, for preparing the springform pan

1 (7.4-ounce, or 210 g) package chocolate chip muffin mix

½ cup (120 ml) 2% milk

⅛ teaspoon ground nutmeg

1 cup (240 ml) water

2 tablespoons (32 g) natural peanut butter or almond butter

1 cup (150 g) chopped bananas

1½ teaspoons sugar

½ teaspoon ground cinnamon

Coat an 8-inch (20 cm) springform pan with cooking spray and set aside.

In a medium bowl, stir together the muffin mix, milk, and nutmeg just until blended. Do not overmix.

Put a trivet into the pressure cooker cooking pot and pour in the water. Pour the batter into the prepared pan. Wrap the entire pan with aluminum foil. Make a foil sling by folding a 20-inch (50 cm)–long piece of foil in half lengthwise. Place the pan in the center of the sling and lower the pan into the pot. Fold down the excess foil to allow the lid to close properly (the pan will fit snugly).

Lock the lid in place and close the seal valve. Press the Manual button to set the cook time for 10 minutes. When the cook time ends, use a quick pressure release.

When the valve drops, carefully remove the lid. Use the sling to remove the pan from the pot and place it on a wire rack. Remove the foil.

Using the back of a spoon, spread the peanut butter evenly over the cake. Let cool completely (the texture will change while cooling).

Carefully release and remove the sides of the pan. Cut the cake into 8 wedges. Top with the bananas. In a small bowl, stir together the sugar and cinnamon and sprinkle evenly over all.

YIELD: Makes one 8-inch (20 cm) snack cake

SERVES 8: ⅛ cake and 2 tablespoons (18.75 g) bananas per serving

Nutrition Facts

SERVING SIZE (65 G)

AMOUNT PER SERVING

Calories: 170

		% Daily Value
Total Fat	6g	8%
Saturated Fat	2.5g	13%
Trans Fat	0g	
Cholesterol	5mg	2%
Sodium	140mg	6%
Total Carbohydrate	25g	9%
Dietary Fiber	1g	4%
Total Sugars	14g	
Added Sugars	1g	2%
Protein	3g	
Vitamin D	0mcg	
Calcium	94mg	8%
Iron	2mg	10%
Potassium	88mg	2%

LEMON-BERRY BREAD PUDDING

You don't often think of a dessert as providing much in the way of protein,
but this one is deliciously packed with 7 grams in every serving!

FOR BREAD PUDDING:

½ cup (120 ml) 2% milk

2 large eggs

1½ teaspoons vanilla extract

1½ teaspoons grated lemon zest

⅛ teaspoon ground cinnamon

4 ounces (115 g) French bread, cut into 1-inch (2.5 cm) cubes

Nonstick cooking spray, for preparing the ramekins

1 cup (240 ml) water

FOR SAUCE:

⅓ cup (80 ml) water

3 tablespoons (37.5 g) sugar

2 teaspoons cornstarch

1 teaspoon grated lemon zest

1 tablespoon (15 ml) fresh lemon juice

2 teaspoons light butter with canola oil

1 cup quartered fresh strawberries (170 g), or blueberries (145 g)

TO MAKE THE BREAD PUDDING: In a medium bowl, whisk the milk, eggs, vanilla, lemon zest, and cinnamon. Add the bread cubes and toss gently until well coated.

Coat four 6-ounce (180 ml) ramekins or custard cups with cooking spray. Equally divide the bread pudding among the prepared ramekins. Wrap each ramekin entirely with aluminum foil.

Put a trivet into the pressure cooker cooking pot and pour in the water. Place 3 ramekins on the trivet and place the remaining ramekin on top.

Lock the lid in place and close the seal valve. Press the Manual button to set the cook time for 20 minutes. When the cook time ends, use a natural pressure release for 10 minutes, then a quick pressure release.

When the valve drops, carefully remove the lid. Using rubber-tipped tongs or a thick dishtowel, remove the ramekins from the pot and place them on a wire rack. Remove the foil and let stand for 10 minutes to cool slightly.

Nutrition Facts		
SERVING SIZE (140 G)		
AMOUNT PER SERVING		
Calories:	**200**	
	% Daily Value	
Total Fat	4.5g	6%
Saturated Fat	1.5g	8%
Trans Fat	0g	
Cholesterol	95mg	32%
Sodium	240mg	10%
Total Carbohydrate	30g	11%
Dietary Fiber	1g	4%
Total Sugars	14g	
Added Sugars	10g	20%
Protein	7g	
Vitamin D	1mcg	6%
Calcium	73mg	6%
Iron	2mg	10%
Potassium	174mg	4%

TO MAKE THE SAUCE: Meanwhile, in a small bowl, combine the water, sugar, cornstarch, lemon zest, and lemon juice. Stir until the cornstarch dissolves completely.

Remove the trivet and discard the water in the pot. Press the Cancel button. Select Sauté/Browning + more to preheat the cooking pot. Once hot, add the sauce to the pot. Bring to a boil. Boil for 1 minute, or until thickened, stirring constantly. Pour the sauce back into the bowl. Stir in the butter and let cool slightly. Top the bread pudding with equal amounts of the sauce and berries.

YIELD: Makes 4 bread puddings, ½ cup (120 ml) sauce, and 1 cup (170 g) strawberries

SERVES 4: 1 bread pudding, 2 tablespoons (30 ml) sauce, and ¼ cup (42.5 g) berries per serving

UPSIDE-DOWN CHOCOLATE-CRUSTED CHEESECAKE

Cheesecake with eggs, cream cheese, sugar, *and* chocolate . . . really?
By using *reduced-fat* cream cheese, a small amount of sugar, and only one egg yolk,
and crumbling a few chocolate cookies on top, you can have it all.

Nonstick cooking spray, for preparing the pan

12 ounces (340 g) light cream cheese, at room temperature

½ cup (115 g) 2% plain Greek yogurt

⅓ cup (67 g) sugar

1 tablespoon (8 g) all-purpose flour

1 teaspoon vanilla extract

3 large eggs, at room temperature

1 cup (240 ml) water

8 chocolate wafers (such as Nabisco Famous), crushed

1 cup (15 g) fresh raspberries (optional)

Coat an 8-inch (20 cm) springform pan with cooking spray and set aside.

In a blender, combine the cream cheese, yogurt, sugar, flour, vanilla, and 1 egg. Separate the remaining 2 eggs and add the egg whites to the blender. Discard the remaining yolks, or save for another use. Purée the ingredients until blended.

Put a trivet into the pressure cooker cooking pot and pour in the water. Pour the cheesecake batter into the prepared pan. Wrap the entire pan with aluminum foil. Make a foil sling by folding a 20-inch (50 cm)-long piece of foil in half lengthwise. Place the pan in the center of the sling and lower the pan into the pot. Fold down the excess foil to allow the lid to close properly (the pan will fit snugly).

Lock the lid in place and close the seal valve. Press the Manual button to set the cook time for 23 minutes. When the cook time ends, use a natural release.

When the valve drops, carefully remove the lid. Let the cheesecake rest for 5 minutes in the cooking pot. Use the foil sling to remove the cheesecake from the pot and place it on a wire rack to cool for 1 hour. Cover and refrigerate overnight, or for at least 8 hours, before serving.

Carefully release and remove the sides of pan. Cut the cheesecake into 8 wedges and sprinkle each with an equal amount of crushed cookies. Top with the fresh raspberries, if desired.

YIELD: Makes one 8-inch (20 cm) cheesecake and 8 cookies

SERVES 8: ⅛ cake and 1 cookie per serving

Nutrition Facts

SERVING SIZE (87 G)

AMOUNT PER SERVING

Calories: **170**

		% Daily Value
Total Fat	8g	10%
Saturated Fat	4.5g	23%
Trans Fat	0g	
Cholesterol	50mg	17%
Sodium	230mg	10%
Total Carbohydrate	18g	7%
Dietary Fiber	0g	
Total Sugars	14g	
Added Sugars	8g	16%
Protein	7g	
Vitamin D	0mcg	
Calcium	81mg	6%
Iron	0mg	
Potassium	145mg	4%

PUMPKIN POT

Made in a pan, but scooped like a pudding . . . this technique keeps things simple without using a lot of pans or dishes. You can find vanilla, butter, and nut flavoring next to the vanilla extract in your supermarket's spice aisle. It lends a butterscotch flavor to dishes.

Nonstick cooking spray, for preparing the pan

½ cup (55 g) chopped pecans

8 ginger snap cookies, crushed

1 (15-ounce, or 425 g) can solid-pack pumpkin

½ cup (120 ml) fat-free sweetened condensed milk

1 large egg

2 tablespoons (30 g) packed brown sugar

½ teaspoon ground cinnamon

¼ teaspoon ground nutmeg

¼ teaspoon ground ginger

¼ teaspoon salt

½ teaspoon vanilla, butter, and nut flavoring or 1 teaspoon vanilla extract

1 cup (240 ml) water

Coat an 8-inch (20 cm) springform pan with cooking spray and set aside.

On your pressure cooker, select Sauté/Browning + more to preheat the cooking pot. Once hot, add the pecans to the pot. Cook for 5 minutes, stirring frequently, until fragrant. Transfer the pecans to a cutting board and finely chop. Set aside in a small bowl and stir in the crushed ginger snaps. Turn off the pressure cooker.

In a medium bowl, combine the remaining ingredients except the water. Stir until well blended.

Put a trivet into the pressure cooker cooking pot and pour in the water. Pour the pumpkin mixture into the prepared pan. Wrap the entire pan with aluminum foil. Make a foil sling by folding a 20-inch (50 cm)-long piece of foil in half lengthwise. Place the pan in the center of the sling and lower the pan into the pot. Fold down the excess foil to allow the lid to close properly (the pan will fit snugly).

Nutrition Facts

SERVING SIZE (97 G)

AMOUNT PER SERVING

Calories: **170**

		% Daily Value
Total Fat	7g	9%
Saturated Fat	1g	5%
Trans Fat	0g	
Cholesterol	25mg	8%
Sodium	140mg	6%
Total Carbohydrate	26g	9%
Dietary Fiber	2g	7%
Total Sugars	19g	
Added Sugars	3g	6%
Protein	4g	
Vitamin D	0mcg	
Calcium	81mg	6%
Iron	2mg	10%
Potassium	177mg	4%

Lock the lid in place and close the seal valve. Press the Manual button to set the cook time for 35 minutes. When the cook time ends, use a quick pressure release.

When the valve drops, carefully remove the lid. Use the sling to remove the pan and place it on a wire rack. Remove the foil and let stand for 1 hour. Refrigerate for 4 hours.

Spoon the chilled pumpkin mixture into individual dessert cups and top with equal amounts of the pecan mixture. Cover and refrigerate any leftovers for up to 24 hours.

YIELD: Makes about 4 cups (777 g) total

SERVES 8: About ½ cup (97 g) per serving

ACKNOWLEDGMENTS

To Dan Rosenberg, my editorial director, whose support and belief in me over the years has blossomed into a strong, forward-thinking relationship—it's fun working with you, Dan!

To Melanie McKibbin, my office manager, who swoops in, handles the office concerns and keeps me and the office in smooth running order. Thanks to your professionalism...and a smile—you add calm collectiveness to the daily chaos of it all! A good chaos, though!

To Sylvia Vollmer, my right hand in the kitchen. Thank goodness you provide eagerness and willingness to be by my side during the longest days that flow over into longer nights sometimes. You're always trying to figure out ways to contribute and conscientious enough to make sure things are "in order" at the end of your day so I can keep going and "function" after you clock out!

ABOUT THE AUTHOR

Nancy S. Hughes writes for a wide range of health and food magazines and is the author of seventeen cookbooks with a focus on low-calorie cooking for weight loss, heart-healthy cooking, diabetic cooking, and cooking with kitchen appliances. She lives in the Mobile, Alabama, area.

INDEX